*TWAYNE'S WORLD AUTHORS SERIES*

*A Survey of the World's Literature*

Sylvia E. Bowman, Indiana University
GENERAL EDITOR

# SPAIN

Gerald Wade, Vanderbilt University
EDITOR

## Ramón de la Cruz

*(TWAS 179)*

## TWAYNE'S WORLD AUTHORS SERIES (TWAS)

*The purpose of TWAS is to survey the major writers —novelists, dramatists, historians, poets, philosophers, and critics—of the nations of the world. Among the national literatures covered are those of Australia, Canada, China, Eastern Europe, France, Germany, Greece, India, Italy, Japan, Latin America, the Netherlands, New Zealand, Poland, Russia, Scandinavia, Spain, and the African nations, as well as Hebrew, Yiddish, and Latin Classical literatures. This survey is complemented by Twayne's United States Authors Series and English Authors Series.*

*The intent of each volume in these series is to present a critical-analytical study of the works of the writer; to include biographical and historical material that may be necessary for understanding, appreciation, and critical appraisal of the writer; and to present all material in clear, concise English—but not to vitiate the scholarly content of the work by doing so.*

# Ramón de la Cruz

By JOHN A. MOORE

*College of William and Mary*

Twayne Publishers, Inc.  ::  New York

Library of Congress Catalog Card Number: 70-153997

# *Preface*

This study aims primarily to evaluate the comic art of Ramón de la Cruz and, secondarily, his impact upon his age, with special attention to the *sainete*.[1] It is an original study inasmuch as I have read all of the sainetes (from here on, the word sainete will not be italicized. The term zarzuela, a kind of musical comedy, will also appear in roman) and other dramatic forms which are cited in this book. I believe that these are representative of his best works. Most of the material not consulted is in unedited manuscripts in the Biblioteca Municipal of Madrid. Since I have been able to read nearly 250 sainetes and about thirty of Cruz's other plays, there is no dearth of primary material.

I have also visited Don Ramón's Madrid—albeit two hundred years too late to meet him there—strolling the streets that he wrote about (most of which have kept the names he used), visiting the church that offered him baptism, spiritual sustenance, and burial, bargaining at the Rastro Market just as his characters did, meanwhile meditating upon the sainetes and Madrid's present response to human nature.

I have sampled the opinions of those who rated him, starting with his contemporaries and including almost every generation from his day to ours, and have formed conclusions which are as honest as I can make them after spending so many hours with Don Ramón that predilections and wishful thinking no doubt have threatened my scholarly objectivity.

What, then, has been omitted? Students of the sainete would have a feeling of greater completeness if someone should continue the work of Durán, Cotarelo, and Kany to get into print the unedited manuscripts and to reprint those works which are difficult to find. No one has evaluated the music of the zarzuelas and other musical plays. This would have only tangential value to Don Ramón's aficionados since others composed the tunes. The principal job remaining, it seems to me, is to exhort people to read the best of the sainetes, for they can be read with pleasure today by people who have no scholarly specialization in the eighteenth century or even in Spanish literature in general, and who do not need copious notes to tell them when to laugh or why.

It would have been difficult for me to have undertaken this study without the bibliographic scholarship of the late Don Emilio Cotarelo y Mori. It is unlikely that I could have finished it in a manner satisfactory to the discriminating public without the loving patience and relentless obstinacy in pursuit of proper form on the part of the Spanish Series Editor, Mr. Gerald E. Wade. My special thanks to Twayne Publishers for making this series possible, to Professors Cecil M. McCulley and Donald L. Ball of the William and Mary English Dept., and to Mr. Herbert Ganter, College Archivist, for their technical assistance, and to numerous friends for their encouragement and interest.

# Contents

# Chronology

1700    Nov. 1: Charles II of Spain, last Hapsburg king, dies. War of Spanish Succession begins.

1713    Treaty of Utrecht recognizes Philip V, first Bourbon king of Spain.

1731    March 28: Ramón de la Cruz is born in Madrid.

1744    Cruz family moves to Ceuta.

1746    Don Ramón's father dies. His mother and family return to Madrid. Ferdinand VI ascends throne of Spain.

1757    Don Ramón produces his first sainete and first zarzuela.

1759    Don Ramón takes a job in the accounting section of the tax office, a position he will retain throughout his literary career. Charles III ascends the throne of Spain. In this year or soon after, Don Ramón marries Doña Margarita Beatriz de Magán.

1762    Birth of his first child, María de los Dolores Carlota. Production of *La petimetra en el tocador*, first really masterful sainete.

1765    Dec. 25: Production of *La plaza mayor*.

1766    Count of Aranda, patron of neo-Classic drama, becomes Prime Minister under Charles III. Period of Don Ramón's concentration upon translations of French and Italian tragedies, comedies, and melodramas.

1773    Fall of Aranda, Don Ramón, released from pressures for neo-Classic plays, increases production of sainetes.

1777    Signorelli's work, *Storia critica dei teatri antichi e moderni* appears with vitriolic attack upon Don Ramón.

1786–    Ramón de la Cruz publishes ten volumes of his works;
1791    answers Signorelli in prologue to Volume I.

1788    Charles IV ascends throne of Spain.

1790    Signorelli, in a second edition of his history, attacks Don Ramón with greater bitterness.

1791    Production of *La Petra y la Juana*.

1792    Feb. 5: Production of *El muñuelo*.

1794    March 5: Death of Ramón de la Cruz in Madrid.

# CHAPTER 1

# *The Historical Perspective*

THE outlook for eighteenth-century Spain was bleak in almost all phases of the national life. The fears that the long reign of the unfortunate Charles II (d. 1700) would end in a war of succession proved justified. The Golden Age in literature and art was dead. The vision of great destiny had gone. Even during Spain's Golden Age, *Lazarillo de Tormes* had shown what was underneath Spanish glitter, and Quevedo, in a deeply moving sonnet, had taken a sad look at the "walls of his country" and found everywhere symbols of age, decay, and death. Waste of men and resources had slowly sapped Spain's proud spirit; the nation was exhausted.

The War of Spanish Succession dragged on for a dozen years after 1700. The Treaty of Utrecht gave France a doubtful victory; victory, yes, because a Bourbon, grandson of Louis XIV, took the throne that the Hapsburg had held for so many years, and thereby started a Spanish dynasty which still today claims the throne; doubtful, because Europe was thoroughly alerted to the dangers of a French-Spanish *entente* and England had seized the Rock of Gibraltar. Where Spain had once dictated in large part the destinies of Europe, the reverse was now the case, and even Spain's vast overseas empire was to become an inert pawn in the intrigues of Europe.

When one looks at the topography of Spain, the arid, eroded plateaus, the numerous scattered enclaves where the people live in rugged isolation, the wonder is that Spain was ever destined to play the role of world leader. Beginning with Ferdinand and Isabella, these resourceful Spanish sovereigns, driven by an all-conquering spirit, had used marriages that were planned to unite nations, and treaties that were intended to be broken. They lacked time to enjoy the laurels won and always pressed on to new challenges. The result was a Spain brought together under

11

Charles I and Philip II of the sixteenth century, developing from
a medieval fiefdom into a vast European and American empire.
This rapid evolution could continue with great difficulty and only
under inspired leadership. The ascent of a weakling to the
Spanish throne would mark the beginning of a long and rapid
decline. The third Philip was that weakling; the fourth Philip
and Charles II completed the decadence.

Philip V, the man chosen to preside over Spain's destinies at
the beginning of the eighteenth century, was a colorless and
undistinguished monarch, dominated in succession by his two
wives, but Spain perhaps fared as well as could be expected
during her transition to a French-dominated culture. The French
cultural invasion did not really drive out the native Spanish
culture; this merely moved into a vacuum. The labors of the
great dramatist, Calderón, the last clear gleam in the gathering
darkness of Spain's seventeenth century, inspired no equally successful effort on the part of other literary men. His eighteeenth-
century successors, Cañizares and Zamora, served by their fail-
ures only to show that an era had ended, with little promise for
the future. Spain needed a foreign transfusion.[1]

As soon as peace was established, the French began their ref-
ormation of Spanish culture. The National Library was founded
in 1712 and the Royal Academy of the Language, almost a
carbon copy of the French "Forty Immortals," was established
the next year. *Diccionario de Autoridades* (*The Dictionary of
Authorities*), perhaps the greatest literary accomplishment of
Spain's eighteenth century, appeared under the Language Academy's auspices. This Dictionary, with its citations from the literary masters to illustrate proper word usage, not only was a vast
improvement in lexicography over what had previously existed,
but finds an honored and useful place today. The Academy's
books on orthography and grammar appeared later in the century. The Academy of History was founded in 1735.

The age of Spain's most intense creativity had ended. The age
of reflection and criticism was at hand. Two names dominate and
symbolize the first half of the eighteenth century: the Benedic-
tine monk, Benito Jerónimo Feijoo and the drama critic, Ignacio
Luzán. Both displayed a cautious liberalism founded upon a
strictly conservative basic frame of reference. The eight volumes
of Feijoo's *Teatro crítico universal* (1726-1739), grounded in

Catholic dogma and common sense, gave food for thought to Spanish minds in many areas of speculation. Luzán's *Poética* (1737) dealt more strictly with literary theory, especially that of drama. It helped to reconstruct drama along lines governed by conservative ideas of the unities. Luzán forms his patterns under the influence of the Italian critic, Muratori, and the Frenchman, Boileau. While forming his ideas on the basis of criteria quite different from those used by Spain's seventeenth-century dramatists, Luzán, unlike some of his contemporaries, was able to look beyond his rigid rules to see some of the values of the plays of Lope de Vega and his followers, but it was quite clear that those in control of dramatic thought in much of Spain's eighteenth century were convinced that the national theater should jettison all traces of the seventeenth-century Spanish influence and adhere to the rules which the French had used so brilliantly in their own seventeenth-century theater.

The prejudice against the national drama of traditional type increased in the last half of the century, the time when Ramón de la Cruz was writing. The political and economic fortunes of Spain, meanwhile, were beginning slowly to improve. The long reign of Philip V was followed by the shorter reign of Ferdinand VI and then that of the able Charles III, whose rule coincided almost exactly with the literary life of Don Ramón. The two last-named monarchs gave Spain the nearest thing to prosperity that she had perhaps ever enjoyed. Modest economic reforms and wise administration gave the country a new sense of stability and a growing middle class. The upper classes, however, offered little literary inspiration. The problems that concerned them were petty and selfish. Most Spanish writers, therefore, using the formulas of classic grandeur, produced works that were artificial and flat.

France was experiencing her Age of Enlightenment, establishing those ideas which were to culminate in the French Revolution, but Spaniards seemed strangely unaware that the Encyclopedists and Bourbons could not long coexist, and so they saw no dichotomy in French influence. The French feel of things, too rational for the Spanish, could not be reconciled with the Spanish spirit, more inclined than the French toward the emotional. When the Spaniard imitated the Frenchman, too often his work seemed trivial, banal, foppish. Pascal might well have been looking toward Spain when he said that the heart has reasons completely incomprehensible to reason itself. The frequent Spanish imitation of French literature was sterile; a French tragedy translated into Spanish lost much of its French finesse and seldom had compensation in Spanish vigor. The elder Moratín, who demonstrated great vigor in his popular poem, "Fiesta de toros en Madrid," failed dismally to achieve a sense of vitality in his tragedy, *Lucrecia.*

One man, and he on only one occasion, was able to combine a French format with a genuine Spanish spirit. García de la Huerta wrote the play of the century, *Raquel,* in 1778, observing the neo-Classic unities, a general sobriety of style, a true Corneillean handling of the conflict between private feeling and public duty, and at the same time, permeating the play with Spanish spirit. Valbuena Prat[2] finds virtue in his balance between the decoratively baroque and a restrained pre-Romantic emotion, a thoroughly Spanish combination.

The tendency in the drama—in which we of course take special interest because Ramón de la Cruz was a dramatist—was for the public to be either pro-French or Spanish traditionalist: the bourgeoisie tended toward the Gallic and the lower classes to the older Spanish ways. The Francophiles, in imitation of the French *salons,* were likely to gather in places such as the Academy of Good Taste or the Inn of St. Sebastian. The opposing groups often argued, and their arguments were sometimes silly. Neither group was producing plays demonstrating creative talent or artistic patience and perseverance. The major Francophiles were Nicolás Fernández de Moratín and Tomás de Iriarte. Ramón de la Cruz soon became the champion of the Spanish traditionalists, although García de la Huerta kept him company.

Madrid was the center for dramatic production in Spain and three theaters allowed the authors to try their talent before the public: the *Caños del peral,* used principally for Italian opera, the *Príncipe,* and the *Cruz.* The Italian opera, given an initial boost by Philip V's second wife, Isabel Farnesio, found that it had to compete with the zarzuela, the Spanish version of the musical comedy. The principal offerings at the theaters during the reign of Charles III, were translations and adaptations of French and Italian plays, Spanish originals based upon these models, Italian opera, and Spanish zarzuelas, rounded out with various short selections called loas, entremeses, and sainetes. Music was more a part of the theater than it had been during the Golden Age. Don Ramón composed almost every type of dramatic production that the Spanish stage offered. Posterity has acclaimed him, however, only for his shorter works.

The actors and actresses who performed in Madrid in the last half of the century were divided into two companies, one for the *Príncipe* and the other for the *Cruz*. The same cast participated in full-length plays and the shorter pieces which accompanied them. Occasionally the two companies would be combined for a single performance. There was of course considerable type casting, but there was a need for versatility too. Most of the players, especially the actresses, were expected to be able to sing. Often Don Ramón wanted a player to cover the whole spectrum of the emotions in the presentation of his roles.

Don Ramón's material usually deals with the people of Madrid during the reign of Charles III. He found that the *madrileños* were able to laugh at themselves. Occasionally he uses characters from the provinces, expecting the Madrid audiences to find them amusing. Undoubtedly they were, but he understood the people of Madrid more profoundly. His major device is caricature, but he means his pen to be honest. As he says, "I write, and truth dictates to me."

The sainetes of Ramón de la Cruz were a sort of caretaker for the national spirit during the time in which the French influence was nominally in control. Don Ramón was ready to lay down his pen at just about the time in which the wise ministers to Charles III were being forced out of their jobs by his son and successor, Charles IV, dominated by his wife and her favorite, Godoy. The French Revolution of 1789 had begun and soon the dormant patriotism of the Spaniard was to be aroused by the outrages of Napoleon. These French excesses and the new Romantic movement in Europe destroyed the Francophiles and restored the true Spanish spirit to the Spanish literature of the 1830's. Thus Ramón de la Cruz serves as a kind of liaison between the two great periods of Spain's literary history.

It has been customary to compare Ramón de la Cruz, the writer, to Francisco de Goya, the artist. The comparison is quite flattering to Don Ramón, for the capacity was never granted to him to depict as Goya did the latter's stark, moving realism. The comparison is not entirely inappropriate, however. Quite often the scenes staged by Don Ramón and those painted by Goya deal with the same kind of people, emphasize the same spirit, and teach the same lessons. It is fortunate that Spain could give to the world both these artists to interpret her life and spirit.

# CHAPTER 2

## Life of Ramón de la Cruz

### I *The Early Years*

DON Ramón Francisco Ignacio de la Cruz Cano y Olmedilla
was born in Madrid, March 28, 1731. His father, called
either Ramón or Raimundo de la Cruz, was Aragonese, from the
town of Canfranc. His mother, Doña María Rosa Cano y Olmedilla, was a native of Gascueña of the province of Cuenca. His
mother's family is the more renowned. Melchor Cano and Agustín
Cano, numbered among the brothers of her direct ancestors,
served the Church and Spain in an illustrious and worthy manner; although the former was the scourge of the Erasmists of
his day, his life was one of conviction and sincerity. Ramón's
baptism, April 2, 1731, at the parochial church of St. Sebastián,
also features his mother's family since the priest who performed
the ceremony was his uncle, the Dominican Fray Francisco Cano
y Olmedilla. His aunt Doña Teresa Cano y Olmedilla was his
godmother.

One of Ramón's younger brothers, Juan, was a designer and
cartographer of considerable note. Among his productions is an
early map of Charleston, South Carolina, but he is best known
for a huge map of South America, drawn in 1775, and for his
two-volume collection of designs of native costumes of the provinces of Spain, completed in 1777.

During his childhood Ramón's family moved to Ceuta, presumably for financial reasons. Ramón wrote his first verses there
at thirteen, and his first comic dialogue two years later. These
early efforts have not survived.

The death of his father at about this time caused Ramón's
mother to move the family back to Madrid. Data about his
formal education are incomplete. He received some liberal arts
training, probably at Salamanca under the supervision of his

uncle, but he did not finish his course. He may also have had
some training in law. It was probably a scarcity of funds that
ended his formal education.

## II    First Efforts at Writing

In 1759 Don Ramón began working as third officer in the accounting section of the National Justice Department at a salary
of five thousand reales per year, and, with one promotion, he
continued in the same office for more than thirty years. Soon after
beginning this work, he married Doña Margarita Beatriz de
Magán of Salamanca. Their first child was María de los Dolores
Carlota, born in July, 1762. One son, born in 1767, was destined for
fame as an artillery general and was cited for gallantry at Bailén.

Don Ramón's childhood literary efforts apparently were few,
since the first works which survive are of the year 1757. These
are a sainete: *La enferma de mal de boda* (*The Girl Sick of Staying Single*), and a zarzuela: *Quien complace a la deidad acierta
a sacrificar* (*The One Who Would Appease the Gods Presents
an Offering*). In a prologue to this zarzuela, Don Ramón presents
some of his ideas on drama, in which, surprisingly enough, he
attacks the sainete—the only form in which he is destined to make
his fame—as a most unworthy art form. He also speaks of the
lack of verisimilitude of the opera, since the aria is likely to
emerge in the most unexpected times of emotional crisis, and a
fifteen-minute cantata may appear just as the actor is in a great
haste to leave the stage.[1]

Don Ramón was apparently feeling his way into the world of
the theater. This first sainete, *The Girl Sick of Staying Single*,
although it does have some elements of farce, is by no means a
foretaste of the dramatic form or quality of the sainete that later
made him famous. The girl of the skit wants a husband. Her
father presents several allegorical figures to propose to her:
music, poetry, dance, and humor. The last-named cures her of her
illness by convincing her that he can make marriage acceptable
to her; the cost to her will be high, perhaps one eye, perhaps
two. Humor is the best medicine, the best recipe for life. It can
be fun; it can be bitter, but in either case it is a kind of thera-
peutic escape. This particular sainete, therefore, although it
serves our purpose as an introduction to what will be his future

work, is not typical in that he soon abandons allegory, preferring to devote his attention to purer farce. He will always stress humor as a medicine for life's problems.

Don Ramón's early efforts indicated his success at working with the musical composers in zarzuela and opera, especially the lighter forms. He established a fine rapport with actors and actresses and thus found staunch allies for his future quarrels over the nature of drama. Rather surprisingly, he was not as critical as he should have been toward his own artistic virtues and faults. His successes at the box office in almost every type of dramatic production kept him from examining his work with a discriminating eye. Furthermore, envious rivals, who were later to pile invective upon him, had not yet discovered the talents of the younger beginner.

The first of his zarzuelas, quite conventional for the period in its structure, portrayed an Arcadian setting with Roman deities. In *Las segadoras* (*The Harvest Girls*), a somewhat later and a superior zarzuela, the characters, while not exactly *majas* of Madrid, are plausible human beings with typical human emotions, expertly manipulated by the author toward an artistically satisfying climax for the piece.

Don Ramón's search for material led him toward the translation and adaptation of numerous foreign writers. His knowledge of French and Italian was quite adequate for his purpose. He utilized the plays of Molière and to a lesser extent those of Metastasio, Apostolo Zeno, and Voltaire. He also did revisions of plays by earlier Spanish writers such as Calderón or Cañizares. More surprisingly, he occasionally utilized plays in English or German, using French translations to work from. Thus he is numbered among those who have translated *Hamlet,* using the French version by Ducis. The translation directly from the English to be made later by the younger Moratín was to prove far superior.

When one explores the early sainetes of Ramón de la Cruz, it is easy to understand his hesitation to devote much time to this subgenre. But he did not hesitate long; soon he saw the dramatic possibilities in the contrast between life as depicted on the neo-Classic stage and life as he knew it, and recognized that the sainete was a good vehicle for the expression of this contrast. His first efforts, as might be expected, do not show the realism and mastery of the art which are to come later. *La fingida Arcadia* (*The Pretended Arcadia*), 1758, for example, is an interesting parody of pastoral idealism. There is considerable dialect, the shepherds sing and enjoy themselves, and the purpose of the sainete, to break temporarily the tension of the main play, is accomplished.

Only a little later, in *La hostería de Ayala* (*Ayala's Inn*), 1760, Don Ramón has reached the point of having some actors represent themselves on the stage while others play regular roles. Gradually Don Ramón makes the sainete—the "filler" between the acts of a full-length play—do what it was not originally intended to do, take the spotlight away from the main production. He accomplished this by depicting characters that, although caricatured, seem so much like the people in the audience that the latter recognize themselves and their fellows, and they start attending the theater to see the selected short subjects rather than the feature.

Thus, as Don Ramón gained experience, he began to feel more and more attracted to the sainete, which he raised to a new level of excellence. His main accomplishment was to make the sainete throb with the daily life of Madrid's middle and lower classes. He wrote for his own time rather than for history, and in doing so, he achieved a paradox which is not uncommon. Often history may reject serious and elaborate gifts proffered her; she may prefer the trifles which are labors of love, rather than sacrifices made in her honor, and Don Ramón's exquisite "trifles" have endured time as masterpieces of their kind.

## III  *The Literary Quarrel*

Eventually Don Ramón realized that he was a part of a literary quarrel which was fought between those on the one hand who sought their inspiration in the tradition of the drama of Greece, Rome, Italy, and France, and on the other hand those who found their preference in the national drama of Spain. This quarrel, if it had been fought on a high plane, might have held far-reaching and salutary consequences for Spanish and European literature. In France the quarrel over Corneille's *Le Cid* and that between the Ancients and Moderns helped to focus attention upon real problems of dramatic evolution. Spaniards might have been taught a new appreciation of the world's master dramatists while realizing at the same time that the Spanish temperament needed its own national spirit and the more or less traditional forms to realize its own dramatic excellence. Spain was not to be so fortunate. The champion of French ideas was Nicolás Fernández de Moratín, who wrote a comedy, *La petimetra,* and a tragedy, *Lucrecia,* which were not accepted for staging because the actors refused to perform. His *Desengaños al teatro español* (*Disillusionment with the Spanish Theater*), 1763, was perhaps the best-reasoned attack on the national theater, but it lost influence because it was conceived in his own frustration and envy. Ramón de la Cruz satirized Moratín in his sainetes. He also engaged in a literary quarrel with Francisco Mariano Nifo in a battle which became increasingly personal, and he soon found Bernardo de Iriarte among his adversaries.

## IV *Political Pressures*

It was not his personal invective that won the battles for Don Ramón. It was the public appreciation of his talent. The recognition of his victory, nevertheless, was postponed by the rise to political power of the Count of Aranda, who tried hard to reform the theater along French lines. A casual reading of some of Don Ramón's titles during the years of the Count's administration would suggest that he had been converted to Aranda's point of view: e.g. *Andrómeda y Perseo* (*Andromeda and Perseus*), 1767, *Antigona* (*Antigone*), 1769, *Bayaceto* (*Bajazet*), 1769, and *Ifigenía* (*Iphigenia*), 1772. It would be easy for those who like to have things neatly categorized to exaggerate the effect of Aranda's pressure upon Ramón de la Cruz. The Count was a powerful and forceful man who loved the theater as an expression of the nation's culture, but apparently his quarrel with Don Ramón was really never a serious one since the latter continued to produce sainetes. Don Ramón did seek his fortune more in the neo-Classic field and less in the sainete than would otherwise have been the case. With the fall of Aranda in 1773, Don Ramón devoted an even greater part of his time to the sainete, and he enjoyed a long reign of popularity in which quite often the two theaters, Príncipe and Cruz, presented different plays of his at the same time.

During Count Aranda's tenure and after, Don Ramón's enemies continued to plague him, though their effectiveness seemed to diminish after 1773. In 1769 he answered his critics in a sainete called *¿Cuál es tu enemigo?* (*Which is Your Enemy?*). In 1770 Don Tomás de Iriarte, younger brother of Bernardo and later famous for his fables, joined the anti-Cruz group at the age of twenty. Others such as Miguel de Higuera and José Sánchez continued the vitriolic attacks. The one which seemed to have bothered him most was that of the Italian critic, Signorelli, whose book, *Storia critica dei Teatri antichi e moderni* (*Critical History of the Ancient and Modern Theater*) appeared in 1777. Don Ramón did not answer him publicly until 1786, when he for the first time published some of his sainetes and other works. Signorelli, in a second edition, replied in 1790 with even greater bitterness. The Italian's ineptitude had reached the point that he could not recognize as parody Don Ramón's burlesque tragedy, *Manolo*.

## V   *His Last Years*

Don Ramón by this time was beginning to feel the weight of his years. Cotarelo y Mori believes that his last productions were inferior and that this probably reflected the poor state of his health. In making this point Cotarelo is forced to conclude that *La casa de Tócame Roque* (*The House of Utter Disorder*) and *El muñuelo* (*The Fritter*), two of his better sainetes, were written some years before they were staged.[2]

On various official occasions Don Ramón was commissioned to write sainetes or other plays. For example, to celebrate the birth of twin grandsons of Charles III, one theater was showing his *Los hijos de la paz* (*Children of Peace*), while the other was staging *Los impulsos del placer* (*The Impulses of Pleasure*). These plays were well adapted to their purpose of pleasing the royal family, but their acceptance attests more to their author's reputation than to his talent.

In his last years Don Ramón was fortunate in having attracted the attention of a noble lady, Doña Faustina Téllez Girón, Countess-Duchess, widow of the Count of Benavente. She and her daughter, María Josefa Pimentel, extended him their patronage. Her influence also turned him somewhat away from the sainete, since he wrote plays to be performed at her home and intended for the nobility rather than for the general public. Presumably there was no thought of restrictions upon his artistic freedom, but he was obviously trying to please her taste and that of her friends.

Don Ramón died at the home of his protectress on March 5, 1794, just before his sixty-third birthday. He was buried in the same church in which he had been baptized, in the vault of the chapel of the Christ of the Faith. This church is still in use.

All during these years of the production of sainetes and other pieces, Ramón de la Cruz continued at his modest government job. He was plagued by financial difficulties most of his life and did not leave his widow enough for his burial expenses. His salary was not large, but it was supplemented rather regularly by the income from his plays and occasionally by the patronage of the Duke of Alva and the Duchess of Benavente. Little can be gleaned from what we know of his family life, since his biographers seldom take us inside his home. Did he and his wife live as the *petimetres* that he wrote about? He could hardly have been typical of the *petimetre*. During the day he worked at his office. In the late afternoons and on holidays he would visit the markets, boulevards, and places of recreation to observe the Madrid scene so that he could spend his late evenings writing. The *petimetres* of his sainetes had little to do but socialize. If his wife played to the full the role of the *petimetra*, surely someone would have told of it. We choose to assume that he was a faithful husband and father, who somehow managed to spend money as fast as he could earn it. Occasionally, at times of illness, Don Ramón had to borrow money to meet the extra medical expenses with a reduced income. On one occasion he borrowed money with the announced purpose of publishing his works, but he was not able to use the money for that purpose.

Don Ramón was small, wiry, and agile. A single extant anonymous portrait suggests modesty in dignity, gentility, and, to Cotarelo, a trace of a picaresque smile.[3] He tells us himself that he was near-sighted. Myopia did not keep him from observing life in Madrid very thoroughly and accurately. He was probably one of those mildly introverted people who seem bolder with the pen than with the tongue, who excel in giving words for others to recite and exclaim.

# CHAPTER 3

## *The Sainetes*

### I   *Introductory Matters*

THE SAINETE is a one-act play. History reveals that this type of drama is better suited to comedy than to tragedy, and that even within the range of comedy, its function is limited. There is little dramatic room for the development of character or for the unfolding of great events. Consequently, to find a first-class writer who achieves his literary reputation from the one-act play is harder even than to find the one who builds his fame upon the short story. It is fine for the master playwright to relax occasionally by writing a short drama, but it is usually in the longer play that he is to prove himself. Cervantes is a partial exception to this rule; if he had written only for the theater, many would have based their estimate of him upon his *entremeses* rather than his full-length plays. As for the sixteenth-century Lope de Rueda, some may prefer his short *pasos* to his longer offerings, but in general only two really significant writers in Spain built their claims to literary immortality entirely upon the one-act play: Ramón de la Cruz and, in the earlier years of our own century, the famous Carlos Arniches. The talent of these men for the short play was obviously exceptional.

The skill of Ramón de la Cruz was indeed great, and this is more or less in spite of a characteristic that would usually be considered a weakness: his sainetes seldom have a plot in the usual understanding of that term. People rush on and off the stage, acting silly or perhaps quarreling. After twenty minutes or so, they suddenly decide that everything is all right and break forth in song. There is little formal coherence. Plot development is not basic to the dramatic values of Cruz's sainetes.

The sainete, as the reader may have gathered, is a rather special type of play or skit. For Ramón de la Cruz it usually represents a series of vignettes structured around a single setting or perhaps two contrasting scenes. The subject matter may consist of a parody of a particular custom or fad which lends itself well to lampooning and the comic distortion of reality. Its spirit is often akin to that of the farce. We have already stated that there is usually little plot structure. The characters necessarily must be easily recognizable types, having little individuality, yet bearing traits that can be brought to light quickly and which seem individualized because of a rare and rather paradoxical combination of exaggeration and plausibility. The characters must be completely ingenuous so that their naive, uninhibited manner contrasts with the sophistication that the spectator likes to think he has.

Many ages have known the sainete under various names. Cotarelo y Mori has sketched the history for us.[1] The Greeks in Sicily called the type *mimos*. Under the Romans it was called *atellana*. The Romans had *mimos* also, but this was given much more to mimicry and pantomime and tended to be more scandalous. Sketches in the *atellana* tradition were written by some of the early Spanish dramatists: Juan del Encina, Lucas Fernández, Gil Vicente, Diego Sánchez de Badajoz. Lope de Rueda carried the tradition to the small towns with the skits he called *pasos*. Cervantes wrote them and called them *entremeses*. By the time of Lope de Vega, the terms used were *loa, jácara, entremesada y cantada, mojiganga,* and *baile cantado y jugado*. As the names imply, the skits had elements of dancing and singing in variant quantity.

With the development of the regular three-act play during the late sixteenth century, the *entremés* became a kind of filler between the first two acts and the sainete the filler for the intermission between the last two. The same terms prevailed during the time of Don Ramón. A similarly short offering called a *fin de fiesta* gave the spectator yet another show for his money at the end.

## II  *A Glossary and Reference List*

Some of the character types in the theater world of Ramón de la Cruz have no direct equivalents in today's society. An introductory glossary, therefore, should be helpful as the reader enters Don Ramón's world. We offer them alphabetically:

*Abate* (*"abbé"*): usually a socially ambitious member of the poor class, he is a man who has taken probationary orders for a career with the Church but has not yet taken his final vows and who may ultimately choose not to become a priest. His position enables him to enter and move freely within upper middle-class circles. He often serves to enliven social gatherings. He serves in various quasi-servant capacities: as tutor or music teacher to the young, as an expert in fashion—advertising a particular merchant's wares for a consideration—, as a scribe, as a secret agent furthering the special interests of any number of individuals. He may hardly be labeled a man of God. Not essentially evil, he is often required to exercise his wits and compromise his ideals in order to maintain his precarious social position.

*Cortejo* has no one-word English equivalent; the usual "beau" or "paramour" of the Spanish-English dictionaries is not quite appropriate because the *cortejo* is fully accepted socially. He may be a lover or just an escort. He is permitted by wealthy men, too old or tired to take their wives to social functions, to serve as escort to these ladies; certain privileges follow as a matter of course. The *cortejo* may enter the home of his lady at all times during the day except for meals. He often decides upon the guest list for her parties. If she is an especially attractive party-goer, he might share his escort duties—and expenses—with other *cortejos*.

*Majo* and *maja*: another term lacking in English, although the dictionaries usually suggest "sport" or "bully." The *majo* (*maja*) is of the lower or lower-middle class, but with special characteristics which seem to represent both the influence of and reaction against the French. A boastful man with a chip on his shoulder, the *majo* is ready to fight on the slightest provocation. The *maja* is also quite quarrelsome and prone to violence if she is provoked or threatened by another *maja*. Don Ramón's *maja* usually sells fruit, nuts, or other commodities in the markets, or she may be a servant girl. His *majo* is apparently unemployed. The *majos* of both sexes are very proud of being well dressed, although one who should see them in a Goya painting might not admire their taste. They seem to have greater self-respect than their economic and social betters.

*Petimetre* and *Petimetra*: Another term poorly translated as "dude" or "dandy." The *petimetres* are of upper middle-class society. They reflect strongly the French influence; *petimetre* is

*petit maître* in French. The *petimetre* is by no means the *galán*
of the drama of Spain's seventeenth century, just as Cruz's com-
plaisant husband who accepts his wife's *cortejo* is greatly different
from the honor-driven and jealous husband of that century's
honor drama. A hundred years hardly seem enough to change a
people so radically. We do not see *petimetres* at their daily tasks.
Don Ramón shows only the hairdressing, the promenading, the
partying, the vacationing. They appear occasionally at the
marketplace. The *petimetre* is normally a bachelor; the *petimetra*,
a married woman.

*Payo* and *paya* ("rustic, peasant") are humble people from
the country who are pictured by Cruz in their visits to Madrid.
Since they are out of place there, they serve as naive characters,
forming something of a contrast to the sophomoric *majos*.

*Usía* (Short for *vuestra excelencia*): This is a form of address
rather than a label for a class type. It is akin to "Your Lordship"
or "Your Ladyship." These people appear only occasionally in
Don Ramón's work. He apparently did not know them as well as
Goya did.

### III  *A Typical Sainete*

The only way for a person to appreciate a Ramón de la Cruz
sainete fully is to see it presented on the stage. Since we cannot
do this, our remaining option is to read one. Therefore, to introduce his sainetes, I offer below and in full a translation of one of
his most admired sainetes. The translation is my own and is
based upon the text of the play *La plaza mayor*.[2]

The translation cannot be an entirely satisfactory substitute
for the original sainete for several reasons: the original play is
in verse; the translation is in prose. The language of Ramón de la
Cruz is very colloquial; it is difficult to recapture in English its
verve, its raciness. The translation is intended to be quite literal.
We recognize that only an experienced playwright can successfully attempt a free rendering in a new language without the
danger of losing many of the artistic qualities of the original
author's style.

There are certain special features of the sainete that the reader
must bear in mind. The style is impressionistic. Often exits and
entrances are not announced, and the dialogue seems to start in
the middle of a theme. While one conversation is still apparently

in progress, the reader's attention may be diverted to another conversation totally unconnected and also seeming to start in the middle. Despite these difficulties deliberately imposed by the author, the reader can grasp a graphic picture from a careful perusal.

Another possible source of confusion in this and other sainetes of Ramón de la Cruz is the system for labeling the characters. The printed version lists the dramatis personae by one of two designations: 1) by character type: *petimetre, majo,* or *mercader* (merchant); 2) by the name of the actor or actress who plays the role. If we learn the character's own name, it is only as it is revealed in the dialogue. This use of the actor or actress to label the role may seem strange until we consider how much easier it is for us in our time to remember the name of a screen star than to recall the name of the character he plays in a typical movie. *La plaza mayor,* typical of the sainetes, has only one scene change; this involves the arrival of the two major characters at the plaza, announced by a chorus. It represents the stroll of two men to and around the main plaza of Madrid, where there is a market, a democratic place to be sure, though somewhat more élite than the Rastro, the market used in another of Cruz's sainetes.

### La plaza mayor (Main Square)

Cast of Characters:

| Actor: | Role: |
| --- | --- |
| Antoñuelo | Dry goods clerk |
| Calderón | Husband of the *petimetra* |
| Campano | Turkey seller |
| Eusebio | *Petimetre* |
| Joaquina | Vegetable seller |
| Mariquita | Vegetable seller |
| Méndez | Fruit seller |
| Niso | Confectioner |
| Ponce | *Petimetre* |
| La Portuguesa | Fruit seller |
| Rafael | Street Porter |

Characters without actors' names:

Constable, Hypocrite (*beata*), Blind men, Child, Maid, *Maja, Majo,* Merchant, *Petimetra, Petimetre,* Remnant Salesman.

(Enter PONCE *and* EUSEBIO *dressed in cloak and hat with wigs. They enter from different sides and* PONCE *passes by.*)

EUSEBIO. Hello, I say, Don Alonso![3] How can you pass by like that without saying a word?

PONCE. I'm sorry, I didn't recognize you.

EUSEBIO. You must have had something on your mind.

PONCE. No, not really. I was wondering what to do this afternoon since there are no plays.

EUSEBIO. Oh Heavens! Is there any afternoon as entertaining as this, just going to the Plaza Mayor

PONCE. You're right; if it weren't for you I would be losing this good opportunity.

EUSEBIO. What we'll do is go together, see all who come, and laugh at everything.

PONCE. We will unless something unexpected happens to us and we lose some pesetas and people laugh at us. Those who go to the fair don't always come back lucky.

EUSEBIO. Come now, you'll never have any fun if you think about the risks. Let's go.

PONCE. Wait a minute. Here comes Teresa, our neighbor's maid. Let's get in a couple of digs on the way.

EUSEBIO. Leave her to me! You'll see how much fun we'll have.

(*Enter the* MAID *wearing a skirt and shawl and in a big hurry.*)

MAID. Do you know what time it is?

EUSEBIO. Where are you going in such a big hurry, Teresa?

MAID. I'm going to take a couple of turns around the Plaza to see if I can find anything good there. I'm in a rush because I asked my mistress for time enough to go to one shop to buy a chemise, and I went first on a trip to the House of Correction, afterwards to see an old lady who has done me a lot of favors and who lives at Lavapiés. From there I went to the Toledo gate to say Merry Christmas to a lady so that she would give me something. She had gone out, but her husband, who likes me, gave me three pounds of chocolate, some wax candles, two dollars, and a box of jelly.

EUSEBIO. Well, you weren't wasting your time.

PONCE. What are you going to buy with all that money?

MAID. Some white silk gloves. And if I can find a nice gold-colored silk remnant from the salesman nearby, I'll make me some classy shoes.

PONCE. Tell me, Kid, wouldn't it be better to buy two chemises?

MAID. Since I have two with good sleeves so that I have a change, I don't need a third one. If a woman has a good pair of gloves, shoes and stockings, a clean shawl, and a well-gathered, full skirt, she is doing fine because on the street only what shows is important.

THE TWO. You're right.

MAID. Good-bye, gentlemen. I don't want that student to see me.

EUSEBIO. We'll be gone, but wait at the wholesale market because we have something to tell you.

MAID. That's fine if you hurry. (*She exits.*)

THE TWO. We won't be long.

EUSEBIO. That girl has a nice build.

PONCE. She does look good from the back.

(*Enter PEGOTE talking to himself.*)

PEGOTE. To think that anyone would go in for literature and not for scheming, knowing how much better off the schemer is with his tricks than the scholar with his real merit. There's no Easter for the wretched, no Lent for the lucky man. Gluttony offers today a thousand invitations to the petition of the rich man and refuses the poor man even the leftovers. A thousand rascals eat on silver, and a thousand worthies on cheap pottery. The attorneys dress in gold and the bailiffs in flannel. They use all the feathers and lace sleeves and hats, and so many who deserve these things do without. What good does it do a man to have brains if he doesn't have the power to use them? But that's the way the world is. Patience! Since I can't taste food I'll go to the Plaza to look and sniff. (*He exits.*)

(*Enter MAJA and MAJO, crossing the stage.*)

MAJA. On the way back we will stop a moment at Petra's house so that she can go with us.

MAJO. We'll talk about that on the way back.

MAJA. Don't forget to buy the raisins.

MAJO. Although you don't have a good memory, it doesn't matter. If occasionally you forget to walk I'll spur you on.

MAJA. Listen, Alfonsa told me we should knock at her window when we go to midnight mass.

MAJO. All right, and I have no doubt that you said you would, since you are so attentive.

MAJA. Of course, assuming that you wouldn't mind.

MAJO. These assumptions of yours will drive me mad, but since it's Christmas, O.K.

MAJA. But Honey!

MAJO. Come on; let's go in peace to the Plaza to buy a little something for supper. We'll work those things out later. (*Exeunt.*)

PONCE. Don't you see what characters pass by?

EUSEBIO. On an afternoon like this, every step gives us enough material for a comedy.

(*Enter CALDERON in cloak and cap followed by a PORTER.*)

PORTER. We've already made four trips.

CALDERON. And we'll make forty if you don't put the whole market on your back at one time because my wife intends to serve a hundred people at the table the way she orders supplies. Watch out!

PONCE. That seems fine to me, Don Antonio.

CALDERON. These are a married man's drudgery, my friends, and although they are annoying there are certain customs that are to be observed to the letter of the law. My wife knows everything about etiquette and she knows that all the guests who attend a *tertulia*[4] at a house during the year are to be invited to dinner on Christmas Eve and to lunch the next day. I don't like to make a bad impression in things like this and so I always get the provisions myself. I may have to return before nightfall for some trifle. (*He exits.*)

EUSEBIO. What kind of income does that man have?

PONCE. A very small one, but even if it were big, the one who loads four big baskets at the market and gives a dance at Mardi Gras time with what he has left over this year, won't be able to afford the next one.

(*Enter the* BEATA *with a little girl.*)

BEATA. Who could have told you, Doña Ana de Zápalos, when you were the wonder of the court because of your charm and your beauty, that the time would come in which you, with all your worthy qualities, would go to the market on foot with so little money and a borrowed coat to get chicory? The consolation that remains to me is that while I had it, I squandered it happily on music and dining and nobody can take from me the good times I've had.

CHILD. Buy me a pound of pears, Mother.

BEATA. You're supposed to ask me that only when you see that I've stopped to talk to people, and if perchance they don't invite you, then you cry and scream.

CHILD. But I'm hungry and hunger doesn't wait.

BEATA. Who could have told you, Doña Ana de Zápalos, that the same friends who stuffed their mouths and pockets at your expense in those days, today slam the door in your face? How badly does one sow without knowing where!

CHILD. Mother, whom shall I ask for a Christmas present?

BEATA. Anybody who stops to talk with us. (*Exeunt.*)

PONCE. Say, do you know her?

EUSEBIO. Yes, but she's so changed that it's a miracle that I recognize her.

PONCE. Well, let's go to the Plaza.

EUSEBIO. Hold on, let's see who is coming.

(*Enter the* PETIMETRA *wearing a shawl and a* PETIMETRE *wearing a gentleman's cloak.*)

PETIMETRA. It's silly for you to come to the Plaza with me; the page would have been enough.

PETIMETRE. He was busy cleaning up the tables, my lady. Besides, I can find out everything that's there with half a turn.

PETIMETRA. For Heaven's sake, don't embarrass me.

PETIMETRE. The way for you to avoid embarrassment is to tell Don Antonio not to begin with his husbandly vanity. Tell him to leave things to me and to the cooks.

PETIMETRA. Oh he won't interfere in anything with you there to stop him.

PETIMETRE. And then, he doesn't understand! He has made three or four trips already and there are still a thousand things missing.

PETIMETRA. Soon you'll see what well prepared salads [we will have]. I've had to set the table for you four times.

(*Exeunt.*)

PONCE. She is the wife of the fellow who passed by earlier.

EUSEBIO. And that other one courts her?

PONCE. Well, who can doubt it? And I bet that he prepares the dinner, serves it with his own hand and washes the dishes afterwards.

THE TWO. Let's go after them for it would be a pity to waste this opportunity. (*Exeunt.*)

(*The Plaza comes into view according to indications given and the Chorus sings.*)

CHORUS. To the rich garden of taste where the earth offers its fruits, the air its birds, and where there is an abundance of meat, fruit, sweets, and herbs. Come, come, come, draw near, prodigals, misers, prudent folk, lovers of sweets; there's business for all at the fair.

MARIQUITA. Cauliflowers and celery.

MENDEZ. Dry fruit and pippins.

CAMPANO. Who will buy a turkey?

NISO. Nougat and jelly.

BLIND MEN. On with the carols; there are just a few left. Come, come, come.

(*Enter the* MAID *and the* REMNANT SALESMAN.)

MAID. Pardon me, do you have a piece of cloth of red gold?

SALESMAN. Here you are, my pearl.

MAID. How much is it?

SALESMAN. Since it's for you, four pesetas.

MAID. How expensive! Will you take two? (*They talk.*)

(*Enter the* CONSTABLE.)

CONSTABLE. God be with you, my Queens.

JOAQUINA. At your service, Mr. Constable. Do you have an extra handkerchief in your pocket?

CONSTABLE. Even if I have a half dozen, they are at your service.

JOAQUINA. Pardon my frankness and have two red cabbages.

CONSTABLE. And how much am I to pay?

JOAQUINA. They're already paid for.

CONSTABLE. Hooray!

JOAQUINA. Take care of Quiteria, who is a good girl and it's a pity that she should suffer for what others don't get caught at.

CONSTABLE. If the plaintiff hadn't insisted, we would have fixed things up already, but we will do what we can. There aren't many cauliflowers, are there?

JOAQUINA. Olalla[5] has the best ones.

MARIQUITA. (*Serious.*) *I* paid a good price for them at the farm.

CONSTABLE. How much are they?

MARIQUITA. One duro.

CONSTABLE. They're hard all right.[6]

MARIQUITA. Buy good ones and cook them well. They will be tender when they're eaten.

CONSTABLE. They're really white.

MARIQUITA. Like milk.

CONSTABLE. And big.

MARIQUITA. Keep your hands off. (*She shakes him.*)

CONSTABLE. You're in bad humor today.

MARIQUITA. Not at all; it's a warning because they get soft if you handle them. (*He goes to another part of the stage.*)

MAID. I'll give you nine reales.[7] If you don't take it, good-bye. Any store has the shoes in pairs.

SALESMAN. Three pesetas is my final offer.

MAID. I'm not giving any more.

SALESMAN. Come over here.

MAID. Quickly, because I'm in a hurry.

JOAQUINA. You mean you didn't give the constable a single cauliflower? You surely are in a bad humor!

MARIQUITA. As God lives, that would be a shame! And you expect me to take it to his house! Look, I owe him four pieces of eight. Besides, the one who gives away his property doesn't need a caretaker.

(*Enter* ANTONUELO *dressed as dry goods clerk with lettuces.*)

ANTONUELO. Señora Olalla.

MARIQUITA. Go away! Constables don't frighten me.

ANTONUELO. Señora Olalla. I'm in a hurry.

MARIQUITA. Make it quick and in cash.

ANTONUELO. My mistress says, how does your conscience let you give so few heads of lettuce for two cuartos? She says these are bad ones and that she wants some good hard hearts of lettuce or give me back the money.

MARIQUITA. Girls, did you hear this customer's harangue? Tell your mistress that while she's earning two pieces of eight, I'm getting two pesetas and I don't get my money's worth in her shop.

ANTONUELO. Come on, tell her whatever you like and give me my two cuartos.

MARIQUITA. Take it.

ANTONUELO. Let's have a bigger coin.

MARIQUITA. What you bet that I grab you by the head and send you home flying?

ANTONUELO. You try it and I'll throw a rock at you.

(*Various people enter and start talking when they reach the front of the stage.*)

NISO. I have fine nougat from Alicante.

PORTUGUESA. Boys, look at my pippins.

MENDEZ. Get your dried fruit while I have some left.

CAMPANO. Here's a thirty-eight pound turkey.

RAFAEL. Who's calling the porter?

BLIND MEN. We have new songs at two cuartos.

MAJA. So, Manolo, you have made up your mind that we're going to eat alone.

MAJO. It's better for our money and our health. Look, you set the table with whatever you have. We will draw up two chairs facing each other. The lamp on this side, the tray on the other and the bottles on the floor. The maid brings the food. We talk a while, we drink whenever our throats get dry or we need to wash our food down. If the soup doesn't taste good, here on the left is the fresh fruit and the dry fruit on the right. We'll drink some *hipocrás*[8] and without shouting or ceremony we'll eat in style. If you want it this way, fine. If not, there are six or eight ways to leave this Plaza. Pick out one and get lost, because I'm not going to put up with any nonsense, Pepa. (*They pass on.*)

PEGOTE. Everything is sky high. A hundred reales is hardly enough to buy a fellow a meal. But my friend, Don Alonso[9] is coming. Let's see if I can stick him for an invitation. Sir?

PONCE. I am at your service, friend.

PEGOTE. And where will you celebrate Christmas Eve?

PONCE. At home.

PEGOTE. That's what I thought. I've been invited to a number of places, but I've decided to dine with just a couple of friends.

PONCE. You are thinking very wisely.

EUSEBIO. (*Aside.*) Get rid of this bore. I just saw Teresa.

PONCE. Good-bye, Mr. Lawyer, we're in something of a hurry.

PEGOTE. He didn't bite. We'll try other recourses and be patient.

CONSTABLE. How goes it, Antoñita?

PORTUGUESA. Hello, Mr. Lesmes, why haven't you come for some pears? I have two dozen set aside for you. Send the boy.

CONSTABLE. This little one will fit in a handkerchief.

BEATA. Who would have told you, Doña Ana de Zápalos, that the day would come when you had wasted so much that you hardly had anything for supper. But my neighbor is with that fruit seller. How much are those sour apples?

CONSTABLE. Doña Ana, I'm surprised to see you.

BEATA. I wanted the child to see all this food. So I came out a little while, but she won't let me because she wants me to buy her something.

CHILD. Mother, I want some dried fruit.

CONSTABLE. And where are you going to carry it?

BEATA. Just enough for her, if you do us the favor; it will fit here in my purse.

CONSTABLE. Well, fill as much as it holds at my expense and excuse me; I have something to take care of.

(*He withdraws.*)

MENDEZ. That woman must carry two suitcases for purses.

PETIMETRA. While we're waiting for Antonio,[10] it won't hurt to take a look for what he is to carry.

PETIMETRE. Here are some fine cauliflowers.

PEGOTE. I was thinking that I had enough time to visit you, but as etiquette doesn't allow me to visit without an invitation, permit me to postpone it until tomorrow.

PETIMETRA. Or the next day, since you have certainly filled your duty toward me. God be with you.[11]

PETIMETRE. Some bore, to try to force himself upon us.

PEGOTE. I don't know how other people manage to eat and dress at another's expense in Madrid.

ANTONUELO. Look at all the things there are here in the Plaza.

FIRST BLIND MAN. There are a lot of people here. Tune up.

SECOND BLIND MAN. Boys, listen, you can be entertained very cheaply; wait.

(*They sing one verse of a new* jácara[12] *that the blind singers have offered as a Christmas present. A MERCHANT comes out and strikes the boy, ANTONUELO, on the back of the neck.*)

MERCHANT. Listen, you scoundrel, you're leaving me alone in the store and you're standing there with your mouth wide open.

ANTONUELO. (*Crying.*) Why are you beating me? Who do you think you are? If I tell my cousin from Postas Street about this . . .

MERCHANT. Go, fine fellow.

ANTONUELO. You be quiet or I'll break your head with a rock. (*They start a struggle.*)

EUSEBIO. Teresa, where have you been?

MAID. I've been around the Plaza looking for you.

PONCE. Here, do you want to go to the play tomorrow?

MAID. Well, sure.

EUSEBIO. But, will they let you off?

MAID. If they don't I'll just take off in big style. I have to go to Mass tomorrow. I'll be two hours; my friend will fight with me. I'll say a couple of nasty things and get fired.

PONCE. But, that's losing your job.

MAID. Well, that's a fine thing! We have Mardi Gras and Holy Week and they, two weeks at the fair. If we work in a place where we don't get time off, we take it. Good-bye, I'll be there at one-thirty.

EUSEBIO. All right.

PONCE. All Hell's going to break loose at her master's house tonight.

CONSTABLE. Be careful that you don't sell this nougat too high.

NISO. No sir, I play fair.

CONSTABLE. Do you have any cinnamon?

NISO. Yes, a very rich kind.

CONSTABLE. How much?

NISO. Take a sample first. (*Into the handkerchief.*)[13]

PONCE. Where are you coming from, Doña Ana?

BEATA. From a church; I've been praying for my late husband.

CHILD. Will you give me a peseta for a Christmas present? (*Aside, but aloud.*)

EUSEBIO. Certainly, my child.

BEATA. Child, for shame! I beg your pardon, sir. Give it here; don't lose it.

PONCE. Would you like something?

BEATA. I'd like a handful of saltwort.

PONCE. Take them for salad, lady, and don't worry about paying for them.

RAFAEL. Can you use a porter?

BEATA. No, my son. I have enough with a little something in my purses. (*Vegetables are tossed to her.*)

JOAQUINA. Are they purses or suitcases?

CALDERON. Follow me, let's see where my wife is. I don't want her to worry over nothing.

PEGOTE. I have seen your wife and since I know that she is having a big banquet tonight, I have told her I won't call.

CALDERON. You acted wisely.

PEGOTE. That's bad! (*Aside.*)

CALDERON. And I would do the same thing if I could get away from home. Good-bye!

PEGOTE. Good-bye. This is what it is to be poor; patience!

MARIQUITA. Don't pass by if you want something good ma'am.

PETIMETRA. And the other fellow was saying that all the cauli-flowers were small today.

MARIQUITA. How many would you like, Your Grace?

PETIMETRA. I'm not a marchioness, my dear.

MARIQUITA. No harm done, lady. Notice, as the other fellow was saying, it's better to err on the attentive side. Shall I choose a half dozen, Sir?

PETIMETRE. Wait until the boy gets here.

(*They depart while others come into view.*)

MAJA. If you want the neighbor girls to come up now that the guitar is strung, they will dance a few turns after supper.

MAJO. You're really asking for it, aren't you? You know that formality is my middle name. I've told you several times that I'm not going to take any nonsense and you get more stubborn. Don't take advantage of my phlegm, today, because the humors circulate, and if choler comes up, I don't know what I'd do. That's enough, few people, a good dinner, fine wine and peace at heart. If you want it this way, we're friends, if not, the Plaza has six or eight exits. Take one and long life to you, because I'm not going to put up with any more. (*They pass on.*)

BEATA. When that Don Antonio was a bachelor, he went to my parties. I'm going to see if he remembers that time. Hello, Don Antonio.

CALDERON. Madam, are you getting your groceries in person?

BEATA. I came from an errand that I trust only to you (*she weeps*) and that, with considerable embarrassment. Do you know someone who will be responsible?[14]

CAMPANO. Ladies and Gentlemen, it weighs thirty-eight pounds and I'll sell it cheap so I can go before it gets dark.

BEATA. How much do you want?

CAMPANO. Twenty reales.

BEATA. Ah, son, it's too much money for a poor old lady.

CALDERON. I'll buy it for you if we can find somebody to carry it home for you.

BEATA. It'll fit here in this purse.

CHILD. What a beautiful bird, Mother!

BEATA. Many thanks!

CALDERON. Beautiful . . . bore!

PEGOTE. The afternoon is passing and I can't find even one person to invite me to dinner. On a night like this am I not to find anything to fill my stomach? I refuse to accept that; these occasions demand cunning since regular science is worth nothing. A wise man in Consuegra said hunger sharpens the wits.

PETIMETRE. How much are the six?

JOAQUINA. Look, they have just paid me three pesetas each to supply a Duke's table. I'll let you have them at ten reales because I'm very anxious to get rid of them.

PETIMETRE. Heavens, woman!

JOAQUINA. Heavens, man! What thin blood! If you're so easily frightened you're no good for war.

PETIMETRA. At three reales.

PETIMETRE. And that's a lot.

JOAQUINA. Do you want cabbage? Here are some bad heads at a peseta.

PETIMETRA. You sows stops being impudent and be grateful that I am who I am.

MARIQUITA. Turn back the clock and light the lamps since her Excellency is passing through the Plaza.

JOAQUINA. You say you want cauliflower, and it may be that you are used to dining on bread soup.

CALDERON. What! This is something to quarrel about?

PETIMETRA. If you'd learn to buy better this wouldn't happen to me.

CALDERON. Well, what do you need?

PETIMETRE. I'll take her home to see if I can calm her down. You settle up and bring a dozen cauliflowers, ten flasks of cordial, ten bottles of Frontiñan wine, four pounds of aniseed and six of almonds, a cask of anchovies, four casks of large capers and olives, and leave it to me that my lady relax and be at ease at dinner time.

PETIMETRA. Count on what they have told you; you're going to know it if you make a mistake.

CALDERON. That devil of a *cortejo*. He prescribes since he doesn't pay. The favor that you are going to do me, Mr. Conceit, is to give more and order less, or one of these days you can leave because nobody is boss in my house but me.

PETIMETRA. But, man!

CALDERON. But, woman! No back talk: You come with me, and you, Sir, get lost.

PONCE. Don Antonio, what's bothering you?

CALDERON. Bothers of a married man who lets his wife take charge.

PETIMETRE. I kiss your feet, lady. Don Antonio, at your service. (*Aside.*) Tonight, I am unaccompanied, without dinner, and broke. (*He exits.*)

(*Enter* MERCHANT *and* ANTONUELO.)

ANTONUELO. Ouch! You're killing me.

MERCHANT. Rascal! I'll send you to Ceuta as a thief.

ALL. What is this?

ANTONUELO. Ouch!

MERCHANT. This rascal has stolen eight pesetas from my cash drawer with a revolver at my head.

ANTONUELO. But, sir, the money is for the nougat.

MERCHANT. It can serve to heal the hole I'm going to put in your head.

ALL. Let him go!

ANTONUELO. Oh, Mother!

ALL. Fight! Guards!

PEGOTE. Now is my chance while the fight's going on.

(*During the disturbance,* PEGOTE *goes along stealing what he can.*)

NISO. Help! They're robbing me, thieves!

CONSTABLE. Stop! What commotion is this?

NISO. Follow that student. He has robbed me of my property!

MENDEZ. He is taking my fruit.

CONSTABLE. I'll go after him and if I do, he will wind up on Carretas Street.[15]

MARIQUITA. This happened because of defending the drygoods clerk.

ALL. Well, get him. Make him pay through the nose.

ANTONUELO. Ouch! They are killing me.

MERCHANT. Turn him loose. He will let go of the pesetas or the devil will carry him away. And since this idea can't really be carried out, discreet audience, it remains . . .

ALL. That for a timely sainete, let it deserve some forgiveness.

## THE END

In this sainete, the exposition is quick, natural, and perfect for the theme. Ponce is bored. Eusebio invites him on a stroll to the Main Square saying, "Let's go to the public market where we will see the countless little dramas of daily life. Life is a stage, and the marketplace is life at its most frank, uninhibited revelation. If you can maintain a detached point of view, people are always amusing."

It is necessary for the two men to express different points of view in order to sustain a conversation, and so the author has Ponce pessimistic and Eusebio optimistic about who will laugh and who will feel the joke. Soon, however, these men fade into the background and other pairs show their comparisons and contrasts. The most interesting and most sustained comparison-contrast is that of the widow, Doña Ana, and that of the student called Pegote. Both are beggars who think of themselves as having a place in society well above that of the ordinary beggar; she, because she was once wealthy and respected, as Eusebio reminds us, and he, because he considers himself an intellectual. In their soliloquies, both reveal their troubles, needs, hopes and attitude toward the world. Other than his being a young man and she an elderly woman, the chief point of contrast is her complete success in filling her purses (which look like suitcases) and his dismal failure. The humor of the purses is cumulative. Surely the audience is roaring when a thirty-eight pound turkey goes into the "purse." Cumulative also are Pegote's efforts to obtain an invitation to dinner. As failure follows failure, his attempts begin to lose subtlety. His pride finally breaks and he is reduced from a hypocritical beggar to an ordinary thief.

Doña Ana is as interesting a character as the world of Ramón de la Cruz holds. She is humorous as the woman who, with the aid of a child, can beg so successfully. She draws sympathy as we learn that she is struggling to retain the vestiges of the pride to which her former social standing entitled her. One must not forget that in her day she was a *petimetra*, an attractive young matron, who gave lavish parties which bankrupted her husband and, after his death, left her destitute. She was more a parasite on society when she was a *petimetra* than she is as a beggar. Finally, she is symbolic of Spain's sense of values: a nation that preferred gold to good farm products or industry, pride in family rather than in personal achievement, prodigality rather than thrift. Doña Ana is not a tragic figure, for she still has her memories and her wits. Perhaps Spain is not tragic either, since her people preserve such dignity and charm, but what disinterested observer can fail to deplore the continued existence of the strange sets of values that Don Ramón has exposed through people like Doña Ana?

A second comparison is offered by the two fruit sellers, Joaquina and Mariquita. Joaquina is generous with her fruit when the constable visits. She obviously wants to be on the right side of the law, but she has a special reason since a friend of hers is in trouble. Mariquita, on the contrary, will not bribe the official.

Teresa, the maid, is pretty and saucy enough to attract the attention of Ponce and Eusebio. Ponce is indiscreet enough to invite her to a play, a circumstance which may cause trouble between him and the neighbor who employs Teresa. In one or another play, e.g. *La Petra y la Juana*, we may pity the poor servant girl, but Teresa would seem to be too brash to need our pity.

A triangle is formed by Calderón, his wife Petimetra, and her *cortejo*, Petimetre. Petimetra is having a large party. Calderón is trying to do the marketing but has already made four trips and

Petimetre is busy thinking of things that the party requires and complaining that husbands always buy cheap products. The relationship of these three requires a certain minimum of mutual respect which normally is maintained. Here, however, the husband seems so subservient that the *cortejo* oversteps himself in his arrogance. When the wife is made nervous by the surly fruit seller, Joaquina, the *cortejo* orders the husband to get on with the shopping while he calms down the wife. The husband must now assert his dignity and he dismisses the *cortejo*. The latter realizes that he has erred and accepts his defeat. He maintains a measure of dignity by the formality of his departure and by making neither remonstrance nor excuse.

One other couple helps round out our picture of Madrid life, the *majos*. The boy wants to be alone with the girl and celebrate the holiday by having a dinner in style. She wants to be with him, but also wants to see a girl friend or two. If he has to put up with feminine chatter, he cannot be the bully, the center of attention that his position as *majo* demands. If she doesn't want it his way, she can leave. He weakens his case by giving her what sounds like an ultimatum—twice. He does most of the talking, but we never learn who wins the dispute. The basic social insecurity of both the *majo* and the *maja* are revealed in their argument. Don Ramón leaves it unfinished, but the best guess is that the *majo* will have to win. She can submit without losing face, but he cannot.

And so, as we have seen, Don Ramón's characters are very real and very much alive. It was not his main purpose to have us study their motivations, how representative they were of their society, or what they teach us about society. Nor does he suggest how to change it to the way he would have it. The play is meant primarily as entertainment for the moment. Nevertheless, the sainetes do provide to a degree these values for the one who studies them, and Don Ramón must have been aware more and more of the social implications of his theater, even though entertainment seems always to be the chief aim.

As in all the sainetes, there is sympathy for the characters but no sentimentality. Every one of them is interesting. Tolerance for human weaknesses pervades the characterizations. Each character is dominated by the role in society that his type has been given, yet each has enough individuality to be plausible.

Sometimes their actions may seem childish to a later and more sophisticated generation, but underneath it all there is the unique Spanish dignity of the individual.

The market itself is very real; the various classes of society mingle quite naturally. Don Ramón usually specializes in fruit vendors, but others do appear for variety. The basic idea comes through clearly that the market square is a stage, large as life, a stage for either comedy or tragedy. For Don Ramón it is a comedy because that is the way life seems to him.


## IV   *Other Sainetes of the Marketplace*

An interesting comparison for *The Main Square*, although of inferior quality as a play, is *El Rastro por la mañana* (*The Rastro District in the Morning*). The Rastro is a market of lower class than the Plaza and there are no *petimetres* in this play. Chief interest here centers upon professional buyers who shop in the market for the benefit of those who lack the time or inclination to do their own shopping. It is rather natural to suppose that these buyers will try to supplement their legitimate earnings by reporting to their employers higher prices and sometimes smaller amounts than they get at the market. In *The Rastro District in the Morning*, these men are Galicians and Asturians. One of them has a young boy of uncertain kinship put in his care and places him as a sort of apprentice with the most successful of these buyers. This buyer, played by Chinica,[16] teaches the boy, Pepe, the shady arts of his business. Pepe proves to be so astute that he not only can follow Chinica's orders, but also make a victim of Chinica himself.

*The Rastro* offers further interest through Eusebio's efforts to find a female who will pay attention to him. His efforts to find a girl, any girl, are unsuccessful, but he seems to take his failure in the masculine enterprise quite philosophically. On the other hand, Simón, a sergeant, has a voice and a manner that reflect confidence and success.

This sainete is unusually full of dialect, so much so that one suspects that Don Ramón wishes to demonstrate linguistic virtuosity as a factor of his humor. The Galicians change their *o*'s to *u*'s or *ou*'s quite often, *l* and *r* are sometimes interchanged, and there are a few other variants. The play also has two Swiss men, as well as a man who incorporates a few French words or imitations, and a woman who speaks broken Italian.

All of Cruz's marketplace settings, especially the Plaza Mayor and the Rastro,[17] throb with the dynamic activity of eighteenth-century daily life. The reader does not need the imagination of the archaeologist to feel that he is living these scenes. The sputtering of activity, first on one part of the stage and then on another, contrasts with the museum-like quality of the plays of Cruz's rivals and epitomizes his genius.

The setting of *El mercado del lugar* (*The Small-Town Market*) serves as a contrast to the markets of the Plaza Mayor and the Rastro. The town's mayor is opposed to having a market because, according to him, the foreigners get away with all the money. If it could be proved that a market would serve mainly to allow the local people to sell things they do not need, it would be acceptable. The solicitor and others argue that a market is indispensable, and by popular demand it is organized. The play's action involves mainly the question of organizing the sellers. One comic character, when told to pay for his concession, tries to hide behind a French accent to claim that he does not understand. A *maja* is accused of planning to sell a great deal more than she has the official privilege of selling. Everyone seems to have his "angle" and, at the same time, to be dissatisfied. It must have appealed to the Madrid audience, who could see that their own markets were better organized.

*Las resultas de las ferias* (*The Results of the Fairs*) serves as still another contrast to the other sainetes of the marketplace, and at the same time, brings us into more intimate contact with those who write and produce plays. The sales people begin the sainete on a pessimistic note by reporting that in the afternoon, sales are poor. Soon Eusebio Rivera,[18] the producer and director, comes looking for a poet to compose a sainete. He meets Chinica who plays the role of a poet, but claims that the people are too well behaved to inspire a sainete. Eusebio says that the people of this fair should furnish material for a hundred sainetes to any poet who stops to listen to them. They listen for a while and Eusebio sees many things to criticize, but Chinica finds reasons not to condemn these people. The humor consists mainly of the contrast between the odd behavior of those participating in the fair and the deliberate refusal of Chinica to consider their conduct other than as normal.

There are a number of repetitions from *The Main Square* in *The Results of the Fairs*: the idea that the marketplace is a natural sainete, the servant girl's telling why for her it is not practical to buy chemises, the use of two detached people to observe and comment upon things that are going on. On the other hand, reviewing his total production, it is truly remarkable that Don Ramón has composed so many sainetes with such little repetition of humorous themes and devices.

# CHAPTER 4

# The Sainete of Character Types

ALTHOUGH the sainete lacks a conventional or formal plot, it is regularly built around a centralizing idea. In many cases this involves a certain character type or an unconventional activity of the character. A study of character types will enable us to learn much about the world of Ramón de la Cruz and about the art of the sainete.

The people of Spain's eighteenth century had a conflicting set of social values. Because certain aspects of their partly Frenchified culture were foreign to Spanish tradition, the Spaniard who aimed at social success had to be very clever in fitting himself into the general scheme of things, into the special problem of being a Spaniard, and into the eccentricities of a system dominated by Gallicized attitudes. The Spaniard of the time of Charles III had the conventional sense of what is right, and he usually tried within his milieu to do the morally correct thing, but beset of course with the same selfish motivations that characterize all human nature. Only between Don Ramón's lines, and then often only dimly, do we see the major moral forces at work in the Spanish environment of the eighteenth century, but we do appreciate how under Cruz's honest guidance we get an understanding of the smaller problems that bedevil human nature. By passing each type in review, we may make ethical judgments about them and their world and evaluations of the artistry of their creator. First, the abbé.

## I The Abbé

Don Ramón's attitude toward the abbé seems to range from hostility to amusement. In *Los hombres con juicio* (*Men with Good Judgment*), he defines rather formally his objections to the type. An abbé asks what is so frightening about his dress. The answer: "It is not what you are wearing that causes the fright;

45

it is you. If you were among those useful sages and well-born abbés whom we venerate because of their industry and talent, no pen or lip would dare attack you. But there are too many abbés in Madrid. Some become abbés to pretend that they are important, some to pretend that they are not loafers, and some simply because the priestly uniform seems best to gain doubtful entry into the drawing rooms and make a business of gaining little favors for themselves or for others. Who do you think needs you?"[1] Since Ramón de la Cruz has been accused of favoring the lower classes, those that gave rise to the abbé, it is well to emphasize here that he does not approve of the priest's use of the cloth for social climbing. The lower-class citizen is favored only if he is content to remain at his level. Although the passage just quoted is removed from its context, the adverse criticism it expresses is quite representative of Don Ramón's attitude.

A typical sainete about an abbé is *El abate diente agudo* (*Abbé Sharp Tooth*). The title is suggested by the abbé's preference for eating lunch at another's expense. His own home can provide him with a broth, but he is hoping to save that for dinner and to get a free lunch hearty enough to see him through the day. He decides to appear just before lunch time at the home of a wealthy acquaintance. As he does so, his friend receives him cordially, talks about good food, especially some trout, and invites him for lunch next Thursday, since the trout is to be available at that time. The friend is preparing to eat out and offers to take the abbé wherever he needs to go. He excuses himself by pretending that he has an invitation from a Countess who lives nearby. He goes to the Countess's home, but she is on a strict diet. He inquires about another acquaintance, a Count. The Countess has heard that the man has been sick. Nevertheless, the abbé goes there, only to find two doctors attending him.

All of these visits take time. The abbé thinks of one friend he may visit and even if he is late, he will be fed, but it turns out that the hosts are spending a week at Aranjuez and servants are sweeping the floor. The abbé is almost in despair of food and so decides to return home for the thin broth that is there. His housekeeper meets him on the street with a man servant who is anxious to have him visit his mistress to advise her on clothing purchases for a suit. The housekeeper suggests that he should have come home earlier since he had not eaten. This forces him to lie that he has. He entertains some hope that the lady who had summoned him has not yet had lunch and is discouraged when he learns that her family has eaten early. At the last moment he is cheered visibly by an invitation to have a nice afternoon refreshment.

There is no hint that any of the people who failed to invite the abbé had intentionally snubbed him. It is just that the life of a poor abbé who must depend upon this parasitical existence is an uncertain one. And we do see him here in other dimensions than his gluttony. In his conversations with his housekeeper, he shows that he has several useful functions for this strange society in which he lives. He is an authority on clothing, has some ideas on sculpture, and does proofreading.

Through this same sainete Don Ramón has a chance to make fun of the medical profession as two doctors are treating a sick man. They send a boy for a cordial; they know nothing of what is wrong with the patient, but they bleed him profusely, and are confident of effecting a cure.

An earlier and less typical sainete on the theme of the abbé and his hunger obsession is *El hambriento de Nochebuena* (*The Hungry Man on Christmas Eve*). An abbé with an enormous hunger finds a friend who is invited to a Count's home to play music for his party. He persuades his friend to take him along to play the bass viol. He plays and sings of food. He sees the food prepared for the feast and conceals it in his bass fiddle. This is not just his own share; it is the whole meal for the party. His deception is discovered and he tries flight. The Count's guests ask the Count not to order him pursued. Don Ramón usually made his attack on abbés more gentle and more subtle than this satire does.

In *El fandango del candil* (*The Lamp Dance*), an abbé has charge of a young boy's education. This boy is apparently in that early adolescent age when he is very unsure of himself socially. The abbé wants him to go to the house where *majos* are giving a party. The boy is reluctant to go slumming and is also afraid, but the abbé insists since he wants his ward to be better acquainted with women, the sex of which the abbé himself is fond.

*La visita del duelo* (*The Mourning Visit*) provides a less obvious satire at the abbé's expense. Here he is very serious and attentive to religious thoughts. One may suspect that Don Ramón

has included him in this sainete with tongue in cheek as if to
say, "See, I do have serious abbés; not all are frivolous, hypocritical, or pathetic." And he seems to be giving a sly wink to
his audience or reader.

In *La civilización* (*Civilization*), the abbé's dress intrigues the
"barbarians" who live at a distance from Madrid and its customs
and who cannot figure out what he is. They specifically reject
the idea that he can be a priest. The satire here is probably
directed less against the abbé's attire than against his behavior.
It is only part of a satire upon the entire structure of Madrid's
bourgeois society shown through the eyes of simple folk who
can recognize genuine values but not the hypocritical trimmings
that the sophisticated use to fool themselves.

The most spectacular abbé of all is *El Caballero don Chisme*
(*Sir Gossip*). Sir Gossip begins by planning his day. It is nine-
thirty A.M. During the morning he will make two visits to ladies'
houses to keep each one informed, secretly of course, of what
the other is doing. He must then scout the stores for various bits
of information, dropping in on someone for lunch. He will then
check the theaters, and afterward attend five dances during the
evening.

Sir Gossip's lackey keeps a page waiting and is upbraided by
the abbé for his lack of courtesy. Showing courtesy to the page
is important to Sir Gossip since servants are his best source of
information. Later Pepa, Doña Eugenia's maid, comes in. He
learns from her that no fewer than five *cortejos* are sharing the
expenses of a party at Doña Eugenia's. Two gentlemen come in,
pleased to find that he has not yet gone to the party. One of the
two has come to introduce the other and to praise the abbé. The
new one, Don Angel, wants Sir Gossip to present in elegant language his proposal of marriage to his beloved at a discreet moment during this evening's fiesta.

Meanwhile Eugenia is awaiting Sir Gossip's visit since he will
judge her costume. He sees the need of some minor corrections
and makes several suggestions. His manner would seem tactful
if it were not so strongly patronizing. At the fiesta, however, the
ladies begin by giving snide remarks, and soon it becomes apparent that in the ladies' war Sir Gossip has supplied all of the
verbal ammunition. He leaves, still aggressive and not at all
humble because of his less than decorous functions.

## II  *The* Cortejo

The next man to pass in review is the *cortejo*. His historical antecedent is the Knight of Medieval Chivalry, whose character was modified by Renaissance neo-Platonism. His major desire is to serve women. True to his knightly and neo-Platonic heritage, he idealizes women, elevating them to the status of an allegorical perfection in virtue. Thus a woman's lover adored her with what has come to be called courtly love, just as the sixteenth-century Garcilaso de la Vega adored his lady love, and expressed his emotion with special poignancy in his sonnets and pastoral eclogues. With a certain discretion the courtly lover paid court to another man's wife, wrote beautiful poems about her disdain for him, kept his distance since she did not requite this love, and avoided all scandal. Garcilaso's poetry is so exquisite that it is hard to believe that he could be an ancestor of Don Ramón's *cortejo*.

The Renaissance and neo-Platonic lover was not really a typical Spaniard, and as the Renaissance gave way to the Golden Age, honor and the good name of the family became a major theme of Spanish drama; as Lope de Vega stated, "Affairs of honor move an audience." It became unwise, at least on the stage, for a man to look at any woman not of his household, for even if she were unmarried, she had a vigilant father or brother ready to react violently to the slightest hint of suspicion.

When the courtly lover reappeared as the eighteenth-century *cortejo* in Frenchified dress, there was no one of Garcilaso's poetic talent to present his cause. There was a man of genius, however, to reduce the courtly lover of the idealistic age to a somewhat more earthy reality; a poet who would have his lover walking on air, then plunged to the ground in the collapse of a mock *hubris* to delight the crowd who remained earthbound. The sainetes which follow illustrate the *cortejo* as Don Ramón sees him.

In *La elección del cortejo* (*The Choice of a Cortejo*), the humorous aspect of the title is apparent immediately since the *cortejo* arrangement is supposed to be spontaneous. A lady named Anarda, who has been married for some time and has never had a *cortejo*, advertises for one. She makes it clear that she loves her husband and only social pressure induces her to seek a *cortejo*.

Various *petimetres,* intrigued by the situation, offer themselves
as candidates. Meanwhile, Anarda's girl friends talk about her
bizarre idea. How will she choose the right one? She plans to get
critical opinion from those who have formerly been "courted" by
the applicants. One of the girls suggests that in evaluating a
former *cortejo,* a girl would not tell of his good qualities, but
would be a dog in the manger and try to keep him from getting
the position even if she no longer wanted him for herself. Another suggested that Anarda is too idealistic, that girls, instead of
seeking an ideal suitor, will "play the cards they are dealt."
Anarda sticks to her ideals, however. She states that: "A man to
whom I am to confide the secrets of my heart must equal me in
birth and exceed me in talent. He must be modest, attentive,
affable, but not intrusive, his conduct so prudent that my husband will never be jealous."

The candidates come to pay their respects. One is too modest
and is sent away for lack of experience. A more sophisticated one
is dismissed as too old and likely to be jealous. An exceptionally
well-dressed one is rejected on the assumption that, having attracted excessive attention to his appearance, he must be conceal-
ing undesirable internal qualities, but all of this seems to be
preliminary for the appearance of the great little actor, Chinica,
who is smooth in manner and words, brings credentials in writing
from hairdressers, doctors, and surgeons, is thirty years old with
twenty years' experience as a *cortejo,* has become penniless in
the service of fine young ladies who have made themselves rich;
in a word, he is the ideal *cortejo.* Anarda then reveals that her
whole idea was a joke. The other ladies do not take offense at
being tricked, but they insist that they do like the *cortejo*
arrangement.

Don Ramón is unusually serious in this sainete. High-level
arguments help establish the chasm between the romantic notion
and the true realities of the *cortejo* convention. The *cortejo* himself is not ridiculed, although his position in society is. The
*cortejo* is almost pitied since it is clear that he can never be all
that he is supposed to be.

A more typical sainete is *El cortejo escarmentado* (*The Cortejo
Who Learned his lesson*). Instead of the serious tone of *The
Choice of a Cortejo,* which resembles a satirical essay, *The
Cortejo Who Learned his Lesson* returns to the normal Cruz

technique of ridicule. Don Atanasio, dressed as an elegant *petimetre*, has aspired to become the *cortejo* of the lovely Doña Leonora. He has bragged to his friends about how much money he has spent and stands ready to spend. He soon finds that serving Doña Leonora is extremely expensive and that her husband, Don Pedro, has borrowed from him a large sum of money. Between expenses and loans, Don Atanasio is beginning to discover that he will spend upon a single night's entertainment all of the inheritance that he had bragged about to establish his credentials as a *cortejo*. Furthermore, Doña Leonora is not treating him in the way that he expects. If he tries to get even slightly personal, she turns very cold. Even as she withholds all privileges of a *cortejo*, she expects him to perform the menial duties of his profession.

A final blow comes to him when she makes public the letter in which he sought to become her *cortejo*, a letter in which he, in language elegant enough for a troubador, sought to serve her, asking no reward for himself and promising to give all in her service. She pretends that she is simply taking him literally. After the joke has run its course, Don Pedro shows Don Atanasio the papers indicating that he has paid all the bills himself, and has returned all of the borrowed money and gifts. Doña Leonora suggests that now that he has been punished for his clumsy manner of seeking to become her *cortejo*, he may have learned his lesson and can probably find someone that he can serve properly in that function. The more obvious lesson of the play is that Don Atanasio's personality is inadequate to his task; he lacks the true self-confidence which the *cortejo* needs. A secondary lesson is that he should have been looking for signs from Doña Leonora that she would cooperate instead of his merely assuming that she would.

It is a part of the convention that a single girl should not have a *cortejo*. She may of course receive incidental attention from one of her mother's *cortejos*. A married woman should not take one too soon. For example, one of the jokes in *El reverso del sarao* (*The Reverse of the Party*) is that a bride has taken a *cortejo*. In this instance the groom is an old man.

The *cortejo* relationship is defined poetically but rather too vaguely in *La civilización* (*Civilization*): "Something beautiful in one's own hands; in the hands of another, something horrible.

Its value to one depends upon its cost to another. It can't be planted because it produces a bad harvest, but it grows wild in the Prado."[2] Stated in more prosaic terms, no *cortejo* can be successful by following a set of rules. There is a spontaneity about the relationship which gives an advantage to the man of good intuition. Thus Don Ramón teaches us that, even as we laugh at the embarrassments of the *cortejo*, we recognize how difficult it is for him to maintain the proper relationship to his lady, to her husband, and to society.

### III   *The* Petimetre

The *cortejo* is a *petimetre* who has maneuvered himself into a special position in which he acquires the new label. If he loses or abandons his position as *cortejo*, he immediately reverts to the more general status of *petimetre*. There are many sainetes dealing with *petimetres*.

In the sainete called simply *El petimetre* (*The Petimetre*), there is a definition of good taste as an instinct which authentic *petimetres* have. (When Don Ramón has an abbé define "good taste" we may be sure that he is mocking the term—or the abbé.) It is interesting the way Don Ramón has captured the self-assurance, the sincere feeling of superiority that pervades the whole man as the abbé expresses it: "Good taste is an illusive quality that lifts the *petimetre* above the crowd, an indescribable spirit which carries him to the sublime." He describes the air with which the *petimetre* conducts himself that gives him superiority, and adds some words about the details of the kind of dress that he needs to enhance his spiritual well-being.

The *petimetre* seems to be oblivious of the fact that the first half of the term in which he takes pride is *petit*, French for "small, little." The *petimetre*, by broad definition, can be any man of the upper-middle classes, but the real meaning of the term for Don Ramón is much narrower since he is concerned with those men who exhibit to a marked degree the conceit described above by the abbé. Don Antonio, played by the actor Calderón in *The Main Square*, is presented as the husband of the *Petimetra;* he is not a *petimetre*. A man who is interested in his profession, his home, his duties as a citizen, in philosophy or erudition is not behaving *muy petimetre*. He must be primarily interested in dress, personal appearance, etiquette, home decorations, and parties. *The Petimetre* shows how the protagonist begins his day.

Don Soplado ("Mr. Overly Spruce") appears in a dressing gown as one who has just gotten up. It is ten o'clock, but he considers this hour rather early for rising. A valet and a lackey are there to help him, and there is a hairdresser who has, the servants report, been waiting for a couple of hours. While the hairdresser is beginning his work, and the servants are supplying the necessary paraphernalia, Don Soplado does his devotional reading. This is obviously a formality, since he stops occasionally to talk gossip with the hairdresser. Three men come in to talk. One is Don Zoilo ("Mr. Carping Criticism"), an abbé who has recently returned after years abroad, and has noticed the vast "improvement" in Madrid in dining habits, furniture, and decorations. Heavy Spanish meals have been replaced with lighter French ones, paintings by Spanish masters with India prints, and the old Spanish beards have gone. As they talk, the *petimetre's* hair takes form, his clothes are put on. He must have enough pockets for several snuff boxes and handkerchiefs, each with a different perfume so that the ladies he meets will be sure of getting their favorite scents.

One of the men speaks about a family who should meet Don Zoilo. In this family one of the daughters sings. Zoilo is not impressed with the idea since he has heard the best Italian music, but he does not pose any objection to their going to call upon these ladies. The scene then shifts to the family where Don Simplicio has the problem of a run in his stocking, but neither of his daughters nor his wife will fix it for him or even lend him a needle. Don Soplado, Don Zoilo, and their companions enter. Each helps one of the ladies to finish her dressing. Don Zoilo sees in the three ladies the personification of the three Graces, while Don Soplado assures one of them that the abbé, Don Zoilo, has learned in the European courts things valuable for the Spanish nation, such as the way to conceal freckles, remove spots from clothes, and wash stockings.

The ladies leave with the gentlemen for mass, but Don Simplicio remains behind. Don Soplado and the abbé have several remarks for those who take religion too seriously; they are considered hypocrites and boors. Here, as in Calderón of *The Main Square*, Simplicio is not a *petimetre*, but a wretched figure. But unlike Calderón, he does not protest. Perhaps the added burden of two daughters who aspire to be *petimetras* is too much for him.

Our special attention in this sainete, however, is upon the ritual of preparing a *petimetre's* hair. It is not merely that the procedure requires a considerable time and the careful attention of a specialist for just a routine day; it takes on the color of a social event in itself as friends come in to converse while the hairdressing ceremony is in progress.

It is in *La petimetra en el tocador* (*The Bourgeois Lady at her Dressing Table*) that Don Ramón lets us see the *petimetra* during the hairdressing ritual that is of course as necessary for the ladies as it is for the men. Doña Agueda is waiting impatiently for the hairdresser. Don Alonso and Don Félix are with her. Beatriz, the maid, suggests that the servants can fix her hair if the hairdresser fails to appear, but Doña Agueda claims that any person with taste can tell if servants have fixed a lady's hair. (In another sainete, *El sarao* [*The Party*], someone compliments a lady's hairdo in public and criticizes it in private. When she asks who fixed it, the reply is, the maid.) Don Félix always agrees with Doña Agueda about the demands of society and the dangers of not measuring up to those demands. Don Alonso, on the other hand, represents in some measure the author's point of view, taking the position that society's demands are excessive. Doña Agueda has fourteen dresses[3] but cannot find one proper to wear unless the new one from the tailor arrives in time.

The hairdresser arrives late because Doña Juana kept him too long. Doña Agueda talks with him about other ladies and their hair difficulties, but soon she concentrates on criticizing the hairdresser's handling of her hair. A process server comes in to tell her that all her property is being impounded pending litigation, but he can hardly get a word in edgewise. She asks him to come back when they are less busy, but for her, both this afternoon and this evening are impossible. The process server leaves. She gets more and more dissatisfied with her hairdresser. Her husband comes in to see about the commotion. Don Alonso, sympathetic to the husband, advises him to leave for his own good. She decides that her hair is impossible and will go out with a coif. The poor French hairdresser tries very hard to please her and still retain a little dignity. We are not told how unsatisfactory her coiffure was for the evening or how the lawsuit came out.

In a century, supposedly of enlightenment, of concentration upon erudition, Don Ramón ridicules the men and women who seem to place such extreme importance upon their personal appearance. In *Las resultas de los saraos* (*The Aftermath of the Parties*), one lady did not go to bed after a party because another party was scheduled for the following night and she did not want her hair disheveled by sleep.

For a woman to be successful as a *petimetra,* in addition to the qualities of knowing how to dress, of how to be a hostess, how to attract men and still keep them at a respectful distance, she needs a husband who can supply her with the expensive clothes, the hairdressing, and the numerous expenses of the *tertulia.* The wife of a tailor and the wife of a hairdresser might covet such social rank since their husbands serve *petimetras.* In *El sastre y el peluquero* (*The Tailor and the Hairdresser*), the wives try to be *petimetras* while their husbands are kept penniless and poorly dressed so that the wives can have a large assortment of fine clothes and can entertain lavishly. The tailor complains at length and without success. His wife shows extreme mental cruelty, presumably without being aware of having a biased attitude. She tells her husband that she is above him in quality, is accustomed to finery, and that she married him only because single girls do not have the social freedom of married women. He is asked to be kind to his wife's *cortejo,* among other reasons, because the *cortejo,* Don Pedro, can bring business to the tailor.

We attend the *tertulia* of the hairdresser's wife. Unlike the poor tailor's wife, she does have one maid. The tailor enters and engages in loud conversation with Don Cualquier ("Mr. Anybody") who is not even acquainted with his hostess and who expresses surprise that she is the wife of a hairdresser. The hairdresser himself appears, wearing a sword. The talk then becomes so loud that the police enter and, when they discover how elegant the wives are and how impoverished the husbands, bring all in for questioning. The contrast in itself was reason enough for police suspicion. It is to be presumed that Don Ramón selected the tailor and the hairdresser as objects of his irony since neither was able to demonstrate the elegance of his profession in his own person although the wives were examples of finely tailored clothes and superbly dressed hair. A similar theme is carried out in other sainetes, for example *Los pobres con mujer rica* (*The Poor Men with Rich Wives*).

The insight that we get into the eighteenth-century Spanish society of the *petimetre* and *majo* is an important part, but only a part, of the contribution of Ramón de la Cruz to Spanish letters. In *El retrato* (*The Portrait*), the particulars of the *petimetra* and her society seem to fuse with the picture of the eternal female and the male's reaction to her. Leonardo, the painter, is waiting wearily for Pepita, the *petimetra*, to come for her final sitting. Finally, Don Lindo ("Mr. Fop"), an abbé, shows up expecting to find Pepita there, and she does appear with her *cortejo*, the Baron. Pepita's portrait progresses slowly because she wants to talk, but it is finally completed; they all admire it, except that the abbé and a Galician servant have minor criticisms. Don Pedro, the husband, arrives and likes it. Doña Pepa is more interested in the views of three ladies: a Marchioness, a Viscountess, and another lady, Doña Julia. They arrive with enthusiasm for the work of the painter. Doña Julia asks whether he is French or Italian. He replies that he is Spanish. They are taken aback at this, and when they focus upon Doña Pepa's portrait, apparently do not recognize it and condemn it vigorously. Doña Pepa, who liked it at first, is beginning to be dismayed. Leonardo is ready to slash his own work. Don Pedro asks him to spare the portrait and promises to remedy the situation. In a speech reminiscent of the *galanes* of old, he asks everyone to compare the portrait with a mirror which reflects his wife: "What human heart can remain insensitive to the fire of these rays, the copy of those rays which mistake what is living with what is painted?" He speaks to the portrait, saying, "you, though mute, say more than the three critics do by speaking." Pepa's friendship with the three is broken up, but the portrait is saved.

An interesting minor touch is that in the early part of the sainete, before the ladies arrive, the abbé tells a story of a couple from Astorga, a town near León, who were so provincial that the husband was always at his wife's side, openly showing affection. This ploy should keep the spectators from being too surprised at Don Pedro's eloquent speech.

In his satire upon the *petimetre* it is obvious that Ramón de la Cruz is condemning the entire social structure since it permits the survival of that extravagant figure. There is no such thing

as a good *petimetre*. Occasionally there are sainetes in which
the extravagance is such that it would be condemned by the
*petimetre* society itself. A good example of *petimetre* excesses
is *Los picos de oro* (*Golden Voices*). The title itself suggests
parody in a way not quite translatable, for the Spaniards in their
wisdom speak, not of a silver-tongued orator, but of one with a
golden beak (*pico*). The pejorative connotation of the word
*pico* shows immediately their opinion of such shallow show-offs.

At the beginning of *Golden Voices*, Doña Elena is being ques-
tioned by her servants for details about parties she has attended.
She tells them that it is not proper for her to discuss these things
with servants. A page enters to announce the arrival of a gentleman. He is sent back to get the name of the caller, Don Luis
María, and is told to dismiss the man. The latter remonstrates
to the servant that he has been sent by Doña Josefa, Doña
Elena's aunt, to deliver a message and so he is admitted. Don
Luis begins to brag. When Doña Elena asks him his errand he
says that it was just an excuse to get in. He then pretends to be
the regular *cortejo* of Doña Josefa. Doña Elena says that she has
never seen him in Josefa's house, so he responds that they have
had a quarrel which has just been patched up. When he starts to
continue his bragging and innuendo, Doña Elena dismisses him.

Soon afterward, two more respectable *petimetres* enter and
work out with Doña Elena a plan for putting Don Luis in his
place. She then receives several ladies, including Doña Josefa,
who shares her indignation toward Don Luis, and Doña Celia,
who remains to be convinced. They agree to hide and leave word
with the servants that Doña Elena is visiting a sick neighbor.

Don Luis soon returns, bringing other *picos de oro* with him.
They decide to start a party with the servant girls while awaiting
Doña Elena's return, and soon slander all of the ladies who are
concealed. The ladies emerge indignant from their hiding places.
Before the men can get over that surprise, the two men who are
involved in the plot enter with masked soldiers. All of the speak-
ers, except Don Luis, apologize with shame and sincerity, and
one offers marriage to Doña Celia's daughter. Only Don Luis is
incurable. He says he is so prudent that he has not said half of
what might be said. He is punished by having pepper sprinkled
into his mouth and having his eyebrows clawed by the ladies.
In passing, we observe that Doña Elena has a carefully worked-out

role as that of one who is to represent the author's idea of proper
conduct in bourgeois society. If there were such a thing as a
good *petimetra,* she would be it.

Nowhere do the *petimetres* seem quite so much in their element
as at the parties. A typical form of entertainment is the *sarao.*
The name, *sarao,* is similar to the French soirée, but it is not
necessarily an eighteenth-century borrowing; we recall that Don
Quixote attended a *sarao* in Barcelona. In *El sarao (The Party),*
several men are promenading along Main Street talking about a
party in celebration of the marriage of an old man and a young
girl. One man says that he does not intend to go since he is with
a friend. The friend takes the bait, saying that the first speaker
should not hold back on his account. The others think the friend
should go also. They brush aside his excuses that he has no invitation and that he cannot dance; they reply that he can amuse
himself just as the author does, by being there and observing
the scene.

The central figure of *The Party* is Chinica, the baton man. He
is master of ceremonies and caller for the dance. His is a very
exacting profession. He must prepare for various kinds of emer-
gencies and contingencies, must know the guests, their prejudices
and foibles. The sainete quickly presents the various types: the
host who is very niggardly and complains about expenses, the
elderly bridegroom, who very quickly gets tired of dancing, the
younger men with subtle compliments to the bride, and the
young ladies with their catty remarks. Probably a large part of
the entertainment value of this sainete is in the music: the blind
orchestra, the duet by two of the girls, and the dances. One does
not have the sense of having completed the story, and then reminds himself that *The Party* is only part one of a trilogy.

*El reverso del sarao (The Reverse of the Party),* the second
part of the trilogy, shows a similar gathering, but from an adjoining room, as if we were seeing a play from back stage. The servants are talking and the blind musicians resting and taking
refreshment. From time to time, the host or one of the guests
comes on stage. The host orders the wine watered down with
four parts of water to one of wine. Our host thinks the servants
are too lavish with the refreshments. It is a rainy night and many
guests are unprepared for the weather. It is very difficult to hire
a carriage. The talk is somewhat more frank, less circumspect

than at the earlier *sarao*, the efforts to flirt with the bride a little
more open. The dance caller has a more difficult time than in
the previous play in his efforts to please everyone; he faints at
a point close to the end. The sounds of minuets off stage and of
some songs on stage add variety to the scene.

Still another point of view is offered in the third of the trilogy,
*Las resultas de los saraos* (*The Aftermath of the Parties*). The
setting is a *petimetre* home on the morning after a party such
as those described in the two previous sainetes. The characters
show the strain of the previous night's partying, but all have the
stoic determination to attend parties the next night as if attend-
ance at these functions were a fulfillment of their obligations as
*petimetres*.

One lady comes to the home of the hostess to complain of the
gossip spread at the previous party and the harm it might do to
her relations with her husband. Various people come to try to
collect money: the landlord who is due eighteen months' rent,
the Galician buyer who demands forty pesos for shopping at the
Rastro for the hostess. Servants from other homes appear to ask
for the return of borrowed clothing, plates, and glasses, and they
request the settling of accounts for broken dishes. The host and
hostess decide that reducing their regular living expenses and
selling their jewels is their only solution for their financial
straits, caused by the parties. They conclude that their situation
is tragic. And tragic it is—though silly too—not because there is
no solution, but because the characters are completely unable
to see that the constant partying is so unnecessary and so foolish.

Like the *sarao*, the *tertulia* comes under Don Ramón's satire.
In *Las tertulias de Madrid* (*The Tertulias of Madrid*), Don Juan
has come home very sick. A servant has been sent to find a
doctor. A close friend, Don Luis, is very attentive to the sick
man's needs; his sister-in-law also helps. His wife, Doña Inés, is
concerned about him, but her guests come in, refuse to let her
worry about her husband, and take over the house, getting noisier
all the time. The hostess can do nothing about it.

The servant returns with a doctor, the first one he can find.
Later, the family doctor arrives. Still the guests enjoy themselves,
ignoring the sick man. The doctors send for a surgeon. Later they
send out for medicine. The report spreads that there is little hope
for Don Juan. Still the merrymaking continues. One guest, with

his mouth full, asks if Don Juan has confessed, but it is realized
that he cannot have done so since he has been unconscious.
Another calls to Don Luis to come out of the sickroom since they
need a fourth for a card game. Doña Inés finally asks all to leave,
but they refuse to leave her alone in such straits. She remonstrates that she is not prepared to serve dinner. This brings forth
a new round of food talk, since she does have ham, coffee, chocolate, and a few other things. Don Luis asks help in certain press-
ing matters. Then the excuses come. No one can lend a hand
although all wish that they could.

When the author has exhausted the possibilities of these social
atrocities, Don Juan appears and reproaches them severely. He
is ill only because of the attitude of guests at *tertulias*. The guests
are properly contrite. It is difficult to say whether such uncouth
people could feel chastised by this verbal spanking, but certainly
the message of the entire sainete is presented with some force.

The theme is reinforced in *La función completa* (*The Complete Function*), where the problem is simply to get the guests
to go home. The lamps have burned out, the hour is late, one
guest is sick. The host is trying to get everyone to leave and,
although blunt, is not blunt enough. His wife, with some reluc-
tance, takes measures to get the supplies to start the party going
again. The doctor (in one version of the sainete, a midwife)
arrives and orders things which require servants to get the stores
opened up to provide what is needed. Other guests arrive, the
entire repertory of the company is on the stage. A song ends the
sainete artificially, but presumably the *tertulia* still continues.

An especially good sainete for the delineation of the stock
characters is *Los refrescos de la moda* (*Serving Refreshments in
Style*). The señora who is preparing for the party has one page
and two servant girls. According to her, six waiters are required.
The husband objects to the large guest list and claims that he
will simply gather his few friends in the gambling room while
she entertains her throng in the parlor. The page and his employers take turns insulting each other. The page says that his mistake lies in serving in homes where vanity is more plentiful
than money. When he is told to go out and find five other waiters
on the spur of the moment, he objects to associating with
Galicians, but he obeys. One gentleman, who just happens to
come in, is asked to be the dance caller and, at the same time, to get

everything else organized. A motley crew of Galicians arrives, all with thick accents and unkempt clothes.

Guests arrive too early. The master of ceremonies has refreshments served with the servants marching in and offering food and refreshment to the accompaniment of a military air. One servant spills his tray on a lady's suit. One lady comments to another that the servants look like vagrants. She then tells her hostess that her servants are unique. One guest, played by an actress new to the stage, is asked to sing. She knows only classical music and is afraid that her song will seem out of place here. An abbé assures her that if it is good it will be appreciated. All seem to like it except the husband, who says he would like it if it were in understandable Castilian. Some then go to the gaming tables, others to dance. The husband remarks that gossip is really the favorite pastime. The sainete ends agreeably.

When Ramón de la Cruz pictures a man of the bourgeois who is not a *petimetre,* the man is usually either quite weak or is unobtrusive. A rare exception is found in *La tornaboda en ayunas* (*Fasting on the Day After the Wedding*). Don Patricio has just married a modest girl named Inés. While he was a bachelor, Pepa, the maid, ran his household. Perico, a servant, asks her how she likes her new mistress. He is surprised to learn that she likes her very much for he had assumed that she had had the ambition to marry her employer. She replies that her parents had been servants of his parents and she felt uncomfortable as an honorable single girl serving a bachelor and so she favored the marriage. Inés appears with gifts and kind words for the servants. She is not impatient to have her hair fixed and even speaks of taking turns by fixing the maid's hair. We seem indeed to have an ideal relationship between masters and servants of the household, and are almost ready to forget that we are observing a sainete. The bride's mother and two sisters arrive with *cortejos.* They start to take over. It seems disgraceful to them that Inés wants to let her husband run things. When they insult the husband and the maid defends him, the mother-in-law sends the maid packing. A *cortejo* is placed in charge of the day-after-wedding celebration. The hairdresser and dressmaker are summoned. Inés is lectured on the importance of showing the husband his place, and the need to spend his money lavishly.

Don Patricio, the husband, enters and immediately becomes

involved. When a *cortejo* pays a compliment to Inés, Patricio
sends him sprawling. Inés, urged on by her mother, tells him
that she is ordering all the expensive things. He tells her of vast
sums of money he has just spent on her for jewelry, a theater
box, carriage, etc., and proceeds to throw everyone out like
money changers hurled from the temple. Inés recovers her position as beloved wife. Her mother and sisters threaten never to
come again. The threat seems welcome.

It is obvious that Don Ramón's picture of the *petimetre* is an
exaggerated one. He was composing farce, not history. We judge
a people, and rightly so, by the literature as well as by the
chronicles. We have only to try to determine how much of truth
there is in Don Ramón's picture. Interesting for the purpose of
comparison is the picture of *La petimetra* in the ill-fated comedy
by Nicolás Fernández de Moratín. He was unable to get it presented on the stage, not because of a lack of verisimilitude in the
characterizations, but because it was not good comedy. In his
play there are two cousins; one is Jerónima, the *petimetra,* the
other, María, a modest and industrious girl. There are two
suitors, Damián and Félix, the former a poor person who assumes
the airs of a wealthy man, the latter a person of means. Both pay
court to Jerónima, but, while hiding from her uncle, they learn
that Jerónima is penniless while María will have a large dowry.
Immediately they can see the tinsel of Jerónima and the pure
gold of María's character. Félix succeeds in persuading María to
marry him and her uncle to accept the proposal. Damián has to
marry Jerónima, knowing that she is penniless, and the old uncle
makes her look even more ridiculous by forcing her to take off
her borrowed dress.

It is not necessary to explain to the reader in detail the defi-
ciencies of the Moratín play. This is our chance to look at the
*petimetra* from the point of view of a man thoroughly opposed
to Ramón de la Cruz in his theory of what drama should be and
in his attitude toward the Frenchified society which Cruz satir-
izes. Moratín too deplores the exaggerated attention given to
appearance by many of the upper-class people of Madrid. He
tries to tell us that among these people there are also people of
sound character like María. He even implies that persons of
money have admirable character; it is the imposters who have
*petimetra* qualities. But he does conclude that bad taste is usually
to be associated with the name *petimetra.*

As we consider the extremes to which some of Don Ramón's *petimetres* go in hairdressing, clothes, and parties, we tend to forget that not all of his *petimetres* are that way. Some, such as the two observers who begin *The Main Square,* are simply cheerful men with enough of a sense of responsibility to seek the path of moderation, which is Don Ramón's obvious answer to excesses. These people presumably are in the majority, but as they are undramatic, they receive only minor attention from Don Ramón.

## IV   *The Majo*

The largest group found in Don Ramón's stage is, as in life, the poor. For Don Ramón's dramatic purpose, the poor, in urban settings, are the *majos.* Any definition of a *majo* will necessarily be distorted by oversimplification, but as we see him in action and live with him, as it were, we will soon feel that we know him well. A good place to start is Don Ramón's own definition or description, found in *El majo de repente* (*The Instant Majo*). Here Don Fabricio, a *petimetre,* is advised to pretend to be a *majo* in order to pursue a girl who has attracted his interest: "Don Fabricio, how amusing you will be dressed as a *majo* with his jacket, waistcoat, and baggy breeches, buckles on his toes and cloak dragging behind, dagger in his pocket and cigar in his mouth: I say, and for picking a fight, what a man with a big spittle shot out like a blacksmith does, you'll leave a fellow trembling."[4]

Along with this costume and this attitude are the proper gestures and conversation. He must brag, of course, but only with a casual air. One of Fabricio's rivals says that he dislikes killing for two reasons: he is not dedicated to population control, and he dislikes giving work to constables and scribes. Fabricio must try to outdo this rival *majo* and two others. He defines what for him is a real man as "One who obeys law and justice with resignation and fights only for his country, his honor, for truth, to avenge wrongs to friends and honorable women; he ignores jokes and pranks, shows valiant disdain for his adversaries, and if he falls in love with the exterior of a lady, plays it cool until he finds out about her material and spiritual values and then goes through mountains and ravines to get her. If he loses he still plays it cool and learns from his experience."[5] We can see, in

some of the more courtly aspects of this definition, a subtle effort
by the author to picture a *petimetre* trying to be a *majo.*

Conflicts between *majos* and *petimetres* may result in victory
for either side. The *petimetres* often invade the *majos'* territory,
Paloma Street, for example, in *Los majos vencidos* (*The Majos
Overcome*), where two *petimetres* on the prowl back off when
the *majos* talk tough. A third *petimetre* arrives and tells them
that the *majos* always retreat when bluffed. They decide to stage
such a bluff and enter a house where a party is under way. The
*majos* send out for their tough guy, but he is easily cowed by
the *petimetre,* who then orders the party to proceed with lights,
music, and dancing. The *petimetre* himself apologizes quite sin-
cerely when he learns that he has been making advances to the
wife of one of the *majos.* He is graciously forgiven.

On the other hand, in *Los majos de buen humor* (*The Good-
Humored Majos*), *majos* and *petimetres* alike suffer when they
serenade two Cádiz girls who, with their aunt, are visiting
Madrid. The boyfriends of the Cádiz girls force four serenading
*majos* and two gentlemen, one a *petimetre,* the other a marquis,
to enter the girls' home and provide music while they dance.
Then they make them undress as if they are going to rob them
(presumably their outer clothes only), and finally tell them to take
their clothes out into the street to put them on.

In *El fandango del candil* (*The Lamp Dance*), a confrontation
is avoided when the *petimetre* fails to challenge the *majo.* Don
Ramón prefers never to show a scene in which there is a fight
on stage.

More interesting in some respects than the *majos* are the
*majas.* The *maja* often is employed and is seen at work. In *Las
castañeras picadas* (*The Angry Chestnut Sellers*), two girls who
are chestnut vendors are constantly exchanging insults. One is
privileged since she has an assigned spot (in a tavern doorway)
while the other must work in the street. Despite their rivalry and
dislike for each other, they share hatred for the *petimetres,* especially for a wholesaler and the people who pretend to be customers but come only to flirt. One of the girls, La Temeraria,
hopes to marry an apprentice carpenter whose master has just
died, but she is realistic enough to know that his mind is on the
master's widow. He flirts with La Temeraria but disappears when
she seems to be having trouble with the *petimetres.* She goes

to the widow's home in a last effort to get her man, but she arrives just in time to witness the announcement of the engagement of the widow, and only seven weeks after the death of her husband. La Temeraria then reverts to her daily quarrels with her rival in the chestnut business.

A spirited *maja* often exerts considerable influence within her own society, but a *majo* usually wins when there is a real test of strength of will. In *La maja majada* (*The Maja Outdone*), we see clearly the essential strengths and weaknesses of the *maja*. Nicolasa is a *maja* with a henpecked husband. She also has a *majo*, Patricio. If this were *petimetre* society, Patricio would be a *cortejo*. Patricio has been seen giving a duck and two packages of jelly to Sebastiana, Nicolasa's rival. It is a hypocritical neighbor who gives her the news. Despite the remonstrances of her husband, Colasa goes to her rival's home and loudly demands the return of the gifts. Bastiana of course refuses, claiming, with some logic, that Colasa has no claim to them. Patricio enters and berates Colasa for leaving her home without his permission. The magistrate enters (he often enters *majo* homes in Don Ramón's sainetes). Patricio explains the cause of the disturbance and announces that he is abandoning Colasa. The latter gets over the shock; having lost her *majo*, she is no longer interested in the gifts, and is even ready to join Bastiana in a party.

Another example of *maja* rivalry is afforded by *Las majas vengativas* (*The Avenging Majas*). The male protagonist, played by the famous Chinica, is named Pocas-Bragas. He is fond of Juliana, but she has no dowry. He is invited to a *majo* party by Paca, who is a sweet nothing, but who has a good dowry. Accompanied by her aunt and sister, Juliana enters her rival's house and, her emotions under control, sings a *tonadilla* when urged to do so. She then proceeds to raise a disturbance, threatening to drag her *majo* and a friend of his out by their ears. Meanwhile, Pocas-Bragas and Paca have slipped away to seek out a priest. Thwarted, Juliana maintains her dignity, accepts full responsibility for causing the uproar, and agrees to sing an encore.

The *majos*, to an extent, do parallel the *petimetre* society in their observance of a certain code of conduct. The same triangular situations exist quite openly for them, and the third member of a triangle operates according to rules which are not written down, but are generally well understood. When the balance is broken because one member of the *ménage à trois* is too strong or too weak, the threesome is dissolved, for the *majo* as for the *petimetre*. The *majos* have an advantage in that their society is not so rigidly artificial. They give parties because they enjoy them, not because of social pressures. A *petimetre* or even a *petimetra* may invade a *majo* neighborhood seeking escape from his or her society. They frequently find a cool reception, but at least they get a release from their own circle with its enslaving conventions and artificialities. On the other hand when *majos* try to dress as *petimetres* (cf. *La pradera de San Isidro— The Shrine of San Isidro*), especially in the clothing of their employers, they have violated accepted limits and will be punished for it.

In Don Ramón's world, the law is rather well upheld. Mention has already been made of the relatively good order at the marketplace while numerous sainetes show personal appearances by a magistrate to restore order when things seem to get out of hand. Appeal is nearly always to reason, and in the presence of authority the *majo* is reasonable. In *El careo de los majos* (*The Confrontation of the Majos*), the relation with the law is the main theme. Since a court hearing is central to the action, its development is largely in the form of a flashback.

Doña Blasa, *petimetra*, complains to the magistrate about a riotous party at the home of Olaya, the storekeeper. The various *majos* and *majas* admit that there was a party and a fight. When some regular guests arrived late and found no room, there was tension. Two *majos*, ordinarily friends, were quarreling over a *maja*. The fight really started when one gave the other a kick in the rear so hard that it sent him sprawling. Two blind men show up as witnesses. After demonstrating that they can recognize various people by their voices, they testify that Doña Blasa also held wild parties and that her principal complaint was not that the *majos'* party was too wild, but that she had not been allowed to participate in it. The magistrate warns the *majos* to be more circumspect in their behavior. This is strictly *pro forma*, and it is clearly recognized as such, since his sympathy is with the *majos*, and he immediately dissolves the case. Doña Blasa turns to her *cortejo* and asks him to find a place for her to move the very next day. The magistrate, however, completely unperturbed, suggests that that same night would be even better.

Occasionally humor can be very close to tragedy. In *El muñuelo (The Fritter)*, it seems that both humor and tragedy are present in striking ambivalence. This sainete, one of the last to be staged, is obviously a sequel to *Manolo* and classified as burlesque tragedy, but like *Don Quixote*, it is only superficially a parody since it delves deeply into the wellsprings of *majo* life with a keen sense of irony. I have chosen to discuss it here with other sainetes about *majo* life rather than in its place with other burlesque tragedies.

Two *majos* who are great friends, Pizpierno and Roñas, are returning from prison; each plans to marry the other's sister. Pizpierno's sister, Curra, a laundress, and Roña's sister, Pepa, a fruit seller, have had a quarrel which was bitter at the time, but they have patched it up. They are anxious that their brothers not hear of this quarrel for fear that it will start a fight between them. They want to be the first to meet their brothers and they discover from Mudo, Manolo's nephew, which gate is the closest to the prison. Mudo ("Dummy") has none of Manolo's bellicose qualities, but he has some of his uncle's fatalistic sense of the demands of honor and vengeance. Perhaps stronger than the blood tie in his motivation is his sense of frustration; interested in both of the girls, they have only scorn for him. He and a friend, Zaque ("Tough guy"), discuss the return of the two imprisoned *majos*. They come upon Pizpierno, who detects a strange expression on Mudo's face and asks him what is wrong. Zaque then says, "Don't tell him and don't let your face give anything away." Obviously Pizpierno now insists on knowing what is wrong and Zaque finally tells the story:

On a rainy night of All Souls' Day, Curra and Pepa were having a feast on porridge and fritters and both girls spied an especially appealing fritter at the same time. Curra got her fingers on it first, but Pepa got her teeth into the fingers. They fought bitterly with Curra on top, Pepa's dress came up and revealed. . . . Pizpierno interrupts the narrative at this point in an effort to decrease the embarrassment, assuming that his sister has mutilated his fiancée. Roñas now appears. Pizpierno really has no hatred or enmity toward Roñas but feels that the fatalistic code of honor demands that they fight to the death. Roñas agrees. The other two leave them alone. As they start to fight they are interrupted by a boy who has bought some bad chestnuts with some bad money, and is running from the chestnut vendor. The boy is defending himself by throwing the bad chestnuts at her. He eats the one good chestnut. Pizpierno and Roñas continue their battle as boy and vendor disappear.

Mudo meets Pepa and Curra and tells them that their brothers are fighting. He reports that it was the chestnut vendor who told them about the fight over the fritter. The women are about to begin their feud anew when Zaque arrives and tells them that the fight of their brothers is over and that both have been arrested.

The district magistrate arrives with constables, bringing the bloody-nosed combatants just as the chestnut vendor arrives, dragging the thieving boy by the ear. She denies telling the story to the two *majos*. Mudo asks the magistrate for permission to leave but is arrested instead. The magistrate questions them all about the causes of the fighting. Pizpierno learns that Pepa has recovered completely from her beating, and with the approval of the magistrate, the four lovers are released to get married. Mudo and Zaque are kept in custody as instigators of the trouble.

Don Ramón lists his sainete as a "Tragedy badly named." From the point of view of the neo-Classicist, it mocks tragedy in two ways: it deals with low-life characters and its quarrel is over an object as trivial as a fritter. Unlike *Manolo,* however, it does not need the concept of burlesquing the fatuous neo-Classic tragedy to sustain it. It is more a mockery of life. As we view it from an age which sees real tragedy in the problems of the poor, the absurdity of the fritter gives place to the reality of the position of Pizpierno. The fatal compulsion to vengeance, though rationally ridiculous, is irrepressible. The piece ends with a clarification of misunderstandings and is therefore a comedy, but by showing how closely related are the emotions of the lowly to those of the high-born, it points the way to serious dramatic treatment of life in the slums.

## V   *The* Payo

Still another character type is the *payo*, the country hick. He lived in or near one of the small towns in the neighborhood of Madrid. The ideal *payo* would have been Sancho Panza. The *payo* was usually naive, though at times his naiveté would be more apparent than real. He did not need to assume the *majo's* pretense of toughness since he seldom aspired to a social position beyond his own.

The most naive of Don Ramón's *payos* are the protagonists Juanito and Juanita in a sainete called by their two names or alternately *Los payos hechizados* (*The Rustics Bewitched*). These two are in love with each other but are not very knowledgeable about the nature of love. Juanito's uncle, a blacksmith, wants Juanita for himself and persuades her aunt to help him persuade the younger ones that love is a fatal illness that needs to be treated with severe therapy. The youngsters do not oppose his views but neither do they accept them. Eventually the older pair see the futility of trying to stop the love of Johnny and Joanie, and permit them to marry each other. In one of the few more daring remarks in the sainetes, Guillermo, the blacksmith, referring to Juanito's denseness in erotic matters, complains that God gives mucus to one who lacks a handkerchief.

There are two interesting sainetes in which the *payos* dress in the costume of the upper classes, not to gain advantage by deceit, but to ridicule those of the upper classes who seek amusement among the *payos*. There is an interesting contrast between the two plays. In the earlier one (1770), *Los payos críticos* (*The Payos as Critics*), the magistrate of the little town of Leganés is awaiting the arrival of the *petimetres* from Madrid, who presumably are just on an outing, and has decreed that the villagers start entertainment to please them. The *payos* refuse to cooperate, and a deathly silence greets the visitors. As they are bored with the lack of activity, they begin to provide their own musical festivity. The *payos,* who have been watching them, imitate their antics humorously. The visitors are indignant at the satire and at the very idea of criticism from *payos*. The magistrate becomes weary of the visitors' airs and tells them ironically that imitation can only be a form of flattery. They leave in haste, and all of the villagers rejoice at their departure.

In *The Payos as Critics*, at least the *petimetres* are capable of recognizing that they are being ridiculed. In a second sainete, *Las usías y las payas* (*The Highborn Ladies and the Rustic Women*), only two years later, they are completely duped. The *payos* are disturbed over the attitude of the *usías* toward their women and plot their vengeance. They have some costumes for a play and use them to disguise themselves as gentlemen. They then engage in important talk about foreign investments, offices, and property, and thus attract the attention of the ladies on the stage. When the latter seem to be following their conversation with complete absorption, the *payas*, dressed naturally, come onto the stage and begin to slap the costumed *payos*. The ever-vigilant magistrate rushes in at the ensuing disturbance and dismisses the whole thing as a joke while the duped ladies retire with considerable embarrassment.

In most of the sainetes about *payos*, the emphasis is not so much on the mockery of the *usías* as it is on comedy with the *payos* themselves and with their daily life. One natural enemy of the *payo* is the soldier. In *Los payos y los soldados* (*The Rustics and the Soldiers*), the *payas* seem to succumb to the charms of the soldiers. Of course the soldiers will soon be gone, but for the time being they seem to have the glamor and style that are lacking in the *payos*. The *payos* are obviously afraid of them. They issue a false marching order for the soldiers. The soldiers are fooled only temporarily, but the *payas* learn their lesson and promise not to snub the *payos*.

In *Los payos en el ensayo* (*The Payos at the Rehearsal*), we have the fun of watching the *payos* as amateur actors. They have come to town to rent costumes from the actors. Their play is one about ancient history, "The Weapons of Beauty," a drama about the ancient Roman, Coriolanus. The rustic who plays the principal role is unable to pronounce the name he is assuming. The amateur actors make fun of the allegory and seem highly amused and amusing as they unintentionally make a farce out of a tragedy.

As Don Ramón does with most of his character types, he alternately makes fun of his *payos'* oddities and draws sympathy to them for the abuses they suffer. Also, like most of the characters in Don Ramón's world, they bring most of their suffering on themselves. Individual lines are often intriguingly amusing. Once a *paya* wishes to express an opinion because she is widely traveled. Asked for her credentials, she mentions several places that she has visited, all of which are within a few miles of Madrid. In *Los payos en Madrid* (*The Payos in Madrid*), two *payos*, tourists, examine the statue of the fountain of Mariblanca and one asks if it is a statue of a saint. The other answers that it is a statue of Mariblanca and remarkable because she never speaks. He ignores the fact that she is stone; he still maintains that a woman who never speaks is remarkable. The old boy had ample reason to think so. He was one day reproaching his wife for not mending his clothes. She replied that she was not his slave and called him *sarnoso* (mangy). He first beat her, then tied her and put her into the well. He eventually brought her up half drowned, but she still called him *sarnoso*.

Despite his understanding of human nature and of the nature of comedy, Don Ramón does not seem to know the *payo* quite as well as he does the urban types. This impression comes to mind when we reflect that individual *petimetres* or *majos* often stand out for their individual activities; with *payos*, it is usually the action of the group. Only occasionally do we get a well-sustained sequence between a pair of *payos* such as Colasa and Patos in *The Highborn Ladies and the Rustic Women*. Colasa tries to quarrel with him, but instead of maintaining her anger, breaks down crying, fearing to lose him, while he maintains a controlled attitude. Since the characterizations are not so well sustained, the plot elements seem unimaginative and at times repetitious. Nevertheless, the *payos* provide an additional ingredient to Cruz's theater and help to broaden our picture of eighteenth-century Spanish life. They probably serve Don Ramón better when they are incidental characters in plays featuring other types. In the trilogy *El peluquero* (The Barber), the first sainete shows a *payo* getting his hair fixed and complaining at every movement by the barber. In the third part of the trilogy the *payo* insists upon having the same barber since he has now been in town long enough to adopt urban tonsorial practices.

In *La presumida burlada* (*The Conceited Girl Mocked*), a widower marries a *paya* who had been one of his servants. She thinks that her new position entitles her to become a *petimetra* and begins to act her conception of the role. She abuses the servants, who knew her when she was one of them, treats her husband as a nonentity, and tries to put on airs for the abbé and others of the party set. She claims to be of the landed gentry, insinuating that she married beneath her. The husband meets the girl's mother, sister, and a friend who are coming to visit. He sees to it that they arrive while his wife is entertaining her fellow social climbers. She tries to exclude them until a more opportune time, but finally has to recognize them. At this point, she is quite penitent, apparently genuinely so. Her family seem to understand that the sudden change of position was too much of a temptation and are ready to forgive. Don Ramón opposes all forms of sham. However, he seems to think that the *paya* who tries to act like a *petimetra* is worse than the *petimetra* herself. Here is one point on which Cruz and the elder Moratín could agree.

Despite their differences in social and economic station, the *payo* and the *petimetre*, as representative of basic human nature, are very much alike in the world created by Ramón de la Cruz. In the play *Chinica en la aldea* (*Chinica in the Village*), Chinica (Gabriel López) takes the role of a *petimetre* visiting a village. He finds the village charming. A native complains of those from Madrid, who, he alleges, seduce village girls with big promises and gentle treatment, but mistreat village men. To him, Madrid is good only for rich people, women, lackeys, and shoemakers. He says further that people grow thin in the city, and in two weeks at the village get fat. Chinica, when it comes to consorting with women, is experienced and freely admits to being one of Venus' knights.

His Madrid friends want him to come back to Madrid to his duties. He says that his obligations are to pleasure and to women, in that order. Asked where he learned this, he replies, "in Madrid," and gives a long list of Madrid's hypocrisies. Paca wants Chinica to return to Madrid since he has made love to her. He would rather stay in the village, and the villagers urge him to do so. Fuentes, a villager, wants him to marry his sister, whom Chinica has also courted. He is willing to be only her *cortejo*. The villagers now want to punish him for his actions and for this attitude, so he is ready to go back to Madrid. Chinica persuades Paca to sing a song which will soothe the irate villagers and permit the sainete to end on a pleasant note.

*Chinica in the Village* is superficially gay but its undertone is one of bitterness:

EUSEBIO. In this little place what can you find?
CHINICA. Freedom, peace, abundance and calm.
EUSEBIO. All these are jewels which are given little value by anyone at court.

## VI  *Allegory*

The various character types presented by Ramón de la Cruz

generally have the virtue of being both individualized and stylized. They present the color of eighteenth-century Madrid at the same time that they expose the imperfections of that society. Normally they entertain more than they instruct. Occasionally there are allegorical elements in the sainetes, but seldom is there sustained allegory. In *El hospital de la moda* (*Style* Hospital), however, there is a fairly extensive allegory which can in part serve to summarize this chapter. An *hidalgo* (nobleman) is looking for a "doctor of customs." He finds him in the person of Dr. Desengaño ("Disillusionment"), and decides to found a hospital to cure those made ill by diseases that spring from subservience to custom and style. One difficulty that he faces is that those who suffer from these diseases do not know, and cannot be convinced, that they are sick. The nobleman then, in quixotic fashion, goes out to round up those who need the hospital's services and bring them in by force. First he sees a *petimetre* couple who cannot speak good Spanish because they are so accustomed to mixing it with French expressions. They are captured and taken to the hospital. Others pass in review; a barber, a poet, a tailor, sick from having replaced Spanish customs with French or other foreign customs. A simple old man is accidentally caught in the roundup but is released. They catch a hairdresser and a seamstress who also have the disease of being Gallophiles.

In a sequel, *La academia del ocio* (*The Academy of Idleness*), the same Doctor Disillusionment and the same nobleman appear, this time to observe that many people follow the wrong occupation and blithely pursue other tasks than the one for which they are trained, always preserving an attitude of flippant unconcern over the unfortunate results of their work.

Don Ramón realizes that the Doctor and the nobleman cannot force reforms upon the people. The two sainetes were written early in Cruz's career (1762) and apparently he came to the conclusion that allegory was not his best outlet for expressing his ideas. He found that he could do better by concentrating upon entertaining the people while continuing to expose the foibles of those who formed this pro-French society. And when the Napoleonic era put an end to the *petimetre* society, Don Ramón had preserved for us a strikingly realistic view of what that society was like in some of its more extravagant manifestations.

# CHAPTER 5

## The Sainete of Daily Life

REGARDLESS of the element or aspect of the sainete that receives major stress, Don Ramón's world (usually Madrid) is basically the same, and the fundamental traits of his characters are repeated throughout the four hundred playlets that he left us. Thus, any attempt really to group or to classify the sainetes in a definitive way is too arbitrary to be persuasive. There are a number that do seem to have as a chief feature the satirizing of customs while still using the same *petimetres*, *majos*, and other personnel typical of Don Ramón's Madrid. Because of their thematic unity, some of these are better plays technically than are most of the other sainetes.

### I  *Leisure*

One of the most popular of Don Ramón's sainetes is *La pradera de san Isidro* (*The Shrine of San Isidro*), so strikingly portrayed on canvas by Goya. The grounds of the hermitage of San Isidro, patron saint of Madrid, rise above the banks of the Manzanares River near Madrid and serve as a fine place to spend a holiday. It would be nice if everyone could take a holiday, masters and servants alike. In one household, the maid is promised the afternoon free by her mistress; the page, by his master. Someone must stay to protect the house, and the master, less wise than Solomon, leaves it to the two servants to decide which one will go and which stay. The page suggests that they should remain together to celebrate, but the girl feels that it is not proper for her to be left alone with him. They decide that both will go, disguised, and expect to get back before the master's return. They dress in their employers' best clothing.

At the hermitage grounds the usual groupings for a sainete can be seen. The fruit sellers are trying to make sales, though

74

their efforts at salesmanship are reduced by the holiday spirit; the *petimetres* are there to flirt, not to buy. A boy selling water is accosted by an old bachelor who wants to drink without paying. The lad calls for help from his friends, who together are able to give the old one quite a thrashing. Meanwhile, the disguised servants quarrel and separate. Eventually, the master sees them both and gives the page a sound beating, but when the crowd asks him for mercy, he relents in deference to the holiday spirit.

Whenever Don Ramón sits down to write a sainete he seeks something that is different from anything that he has previously written. As the fertile dramatic poet of the eighteenth century, he has something of the same problem which confronted Lope de Vega a century and a half earlier. Changing the names of the actors, changing the settings, even changing the action does not necessarily give the spectator or reader something fundamentally new. Don Ramón has human nature and his own comical approach to it, as well as special artificialities which develop from the contrasts originating in a Spanish society dominated by French ways. Each new play does seem to have a somewhat different setting or a slightly different atmosphere.

In the evenings a common pastime is for the citizens of Madrid to take a stroll along the Prado, the main north-south avenue of Madrid, the street close to the Retiro Park. Thus it is a logical setting for *El prado por la noche* (*The Prado at Night*). The usual groups are there: the blind singers, the isolated beggar, the women selling fruit, a *payo* and his wife. The story, such as it is, centers around three pairs: a couple of somewhat elderly men, their younger wives, and two *petimetres*. The wives do not want to go strolling with their husbands. They arrange to meet the *petimetres* "by chance." As the sainete is about to end and we are ready to accept the idea that the husbands have been deceived, one of them recites a sonnet about the *Prado* which sums up the theme of the sainete, saying that in search of pleasure, men and women get involved in all sorts of intrigues with various pretexts at great risks to their reputations. There is a subtlety about this ending since we do not know whether the sonneteer is being clever about human nature and duped about his own wife or whether he is including himself and his wife in the general satire and accepting stoically something that he cannot prevent.

*La fiesta de pólvora* (*The Fireworks*) is a typical sainete of daily life in Madrid, featuring a special event. Numerous groups gather where the fireworks are to be and the groups exhibit different idiosyncrasies just as in the sainetes of the marketplace. One man has an obsession about the night air. He wants his wife to dress warmly and looks for sheltered spots although the night is warm and there is no sign of a breeze. One person asks in his presence, "Do you know what day in January it is?" There is a quarrel about the right to occupy a certain bench strategically placed for viewing the fireworks. The first arrivals have already moved close to one another to make room for as many as possible, when a person arrives who claims to have paid for the use of the bench. One of the seated men is ready to dispute this claim with his fists, but his wife talks him out of it and they move. An abbé comes, accompanied by a servant lighting the way with a torch. Everyone wants darkness and so they force him to put out the light. A trio of supposedly blind musicians is present to try to pick up some money. One is a boy singer who is not blind and at least one of the others has some vision. One father has to lift his daughter so that she can see above the crowd. Stage directions call for skyrockets to be shown. When the fireworks are over, so is the sainete.

Rather similar is *La retreta* (*The Retreat*). One man is trying to mail a letter. Actually he is using this as an excuse to talk to the girls that attract him. Another man has a letter which he has difficulty reading. We are led to believe, first that he has trouble reading because of lack of light, then that the problem is poor penmanship; finally, we learn that the man cannot read. Others appear on various missions, usually trying to get into conversations with attractive strangers of the opposite sex.

Several sainetes feature some aspect of Christmas. One such is *Las superfluidades* (*Superfluities*). Here the excesses are connected with the formalities of celebrating Christmas. One cause of the holiday frenzy is simply getting to see people to wish them the season's greetings. One man seeking people to greet suffers so from asthma that he should be in bed. Another is so absent-minded that he keeps returning to the same people to give his prepared speech. One man uses five reams of paper mailing his greetings and is ready to use five more. One of the people that he thinks he should send greetings to is the mayor of the nearby village of Illescas; he cannot recall the name. Others send servants all over town delivering greetings. Various other formalities are involved. If two people of different social classes deal with each other on a regular basis, the one of the higher rank should give a Christmas gift to the other. If the giver approaches the receiver his gift may be a small one. If he is approached by the receiver the gift is to be more substantial. One person eagerly seeks those on whom he is to bestow charity, but it is obvious that self-interest determines his zeal. The Mass, of course, is an essential for Christmas day, but it is just another duty to be observed for fear of criticism if one omits the observance. Every act seems superfluous because the spirit is missing.

*The Superfluities* also stresses religious hypocrisy. One *petimetra*, Doña Juana, gave an elaborate dinner party for Christmas Eve. She called it a *colación* ("snack") because it was a fast day and a full meal presumably was prohibited. But according to the report, it was anything but a snack. The salad was rich and plentiful. Huge quantities of fish were served. "And turkey?" someone asked. "Of course not, this is a Christian community." Numerous people found that in the frenzy of exchanging season's greetings, they suffered stomach pains. One lady was reported to have vomited two whole fish which seemed not to have suffered at all from her teeth or her digestive system. No one thinks of the season as the time to rest, to meditate or to relax. Relaxing time comes at the end when the weary but faithful celebrant has the consolation of having properly wished everyone the season's greetings.

## II   *Inns and Bars*

There are a number of plays about inns, a factor that causes no surprise when we consider the possibilities of getting strangers together in a setting in which they are likely to be least inhibited. In such plays the innkeeper and his wife have difficult jobs since they must be tyrants toward some and obsequious servants for others. Furthermore, the tourist trade in eighteenth-century Spain was uncertain at best and filled with dangers. In *Las gitanillas* (*The Gypsy Girls*), the innkeeper and his wife are about to go bankrupt for lack of customers, she lamenting the success of a rival inn and he intimating that the rival exploits sex. A large troop of gypsies comes in and takes over. Two magistrates arrive. The gypsies flatter these officials, then steal their watches and snuff boxes. A messenger arrives with a legal paper denouncing the gypsies as thieves. The gypsies return the stolen goods, ask for mercy, and promise to leave the area. The physical attractiveness and beautiful songs of the girl gypsies soften the magistrates' ire and they let them go.

A more typical sainete about inns is *La mesón en Navidad* (*The Inn at Christmas Time*). It features a large number of actors representing different social classes: a modest *corregidor* (governor)[1] and his very conceited wife, a marquis, a sexton, muleteers, and peasants. Life would seem serene except that the governor's wife complains that she is not being treated with proper deference. Although she and her husband have just arrived, she wants to leave, but her driver refuses to budge because it is cold outside and he does not believe that accommodations will be better at the next inn. For entertainment there are Valencian girls who can be persuaded to sing. The governor's wife announces that she will be content to remain if her seat in the audience is even slightly better than that of the others. A village magistrate enters, and it is soon obvious that he has neither the physical appearance nor the moral force to execute his job. He is a front man for a notary who has the real power in the village. Presumably he serves as a contrast to the governor's wife who is overly assertive about rank. The innkeeper has no food except bread, but the muleteers have an abundance of everything. One person suggests that this bizarre society takes on equality in the loneliness of an inn on a winter night, that they will again assume their accustomed roles when they leave. It is a sort of reversal of the medieval dance of death theme which proclaims that all differences of status are temporary, pending the arrival of the great equalizer, Death.

Somewhat longer than the typical sainete and listed as a *fin de fiesta* is *La botillería* (*The Bar*), a special place of refreshment and entertainment in eighteenth-century Madrid. Some of the things available there sound strangely modern: soft drinks, sherbets of numerous flavors, ice cream. The characters in this play seem of somewhat humbler social rank than in some others. One of the leading characters admits that his wife has gotten the upper hand and his friend advises patience as the only recourse. As they talk about the *botillería*, they decide that it is a good place to hear and participate in conversation and to learn how to behave since both good and bad manners are on display. Unlike those in certain other gatherings, these conversations revolve around problems of everyday life, not political theories and other forms of more elevated discourse. Masks and other disguises prevent recognitions until the author is ready for them. A man and a woman enter, and from the conversation it is obvious that she is preoccupied with her health. She speaks with humorous irrationality of things to do and to avoid for health's sake: e.g., knitting, as this is bad for the hips. A man comes in; his conversation is about his wife's health. According to him, her health prevents her from doing distasteful things early in the day, but would never interrupt her enjoyment of a play. Eventually this man discovers that the woman previously referred to is his wife. He starts a quarrel with her escort, but the owner has a persuasive bouncer eject them and the play ends quickly.

## III  *Extravagance*

It is not often that Don Ramón needs three sainetes to develop a single theme, but a custom can be so dominatingly all-pervasive at times that he devotes a series of three to emphasize the wrong. In the Barber's trilogy, the theme concerns the extravagantly expensive customs involved in a wedding and the elaborate party that follows it. The first play has Manuel, an apprentice barber, decide to get married despite the fact that Diego, the master barber, has been completely cowed by his wife. A strong inducement for Manuel is the hundred-ducat dowry that the girl has. Manuel shows that he has some shrewdness by openly flattering *la maestra* (Diego's wife).

The second part of the trilogy features the wedding and wedding feast. It must be made an important affair. The bride's aunt has a house too small for proper celebration and so the home of the master barber is selected and he is given *carte blanche* for defraying the expenses, knowing the size of the dowry. The groom continues to flatter the *maestra* but does not notice that his bride's aunt is losing her temper. A quarrel ensues between the *maestra* and the aunt. This mars the scene of marital bliss. It is, alas, only the prelude. Manuel discovers that the entire dowry must go to meet the expenses of the wedding day and evening, for nothing has been spared: coach and horsemen, musicians,

food—everything is first class. The groom demands that the
master barber at least share the expenses with him, but no, the
master barber has no funds; he is just beginning to get on his
feet financially after the expense of his own wedding many years
before.

In the third part of the trilogy, the *maestra* has died from
causes which mystified the doctors. The henpecked husband finds
no relief; in fact things are now far worse. The bride and groom
are living with him. She has brought her two younger sisters
with her and, still smarting over the loss of her fortune, dominates the household far more thoroughly than the *maestra* ever
did. The new apprentice has no respect for his master and says
that the latter is more apprentice than he. The widower decides
that the only way he can recover his dignity is to remarry. An
eligible candidate appears, the cousin of a friend of his. The old
widower hesitates since the girl has no dowry and he really
should have twice as expensive a wedding the second time, but
he is so desperate to get rid of his oppressor that he decides to
go through with it. Finally, with the intervention of the magistrate, Manuel and his wife are put out of the widower's house.
There is no hint that the new *maestra* will become a tyrant,
because Don Ramón always likes a sainete to end on an optimistic note where possible. Diego rehires Manuel, confident that
everything will turn out fine.

In terms of the economic status of the laboring man, the custom of the big wedding is almost tragic. An analogous extravagance among the *petimetres*, while not tragic, is certainly serious.
In *Los novios espantados* (*The Frightened Fiancés*), two young
cousins are preparing to attend a dance with their prospective
*fiancés*. The entire sainete centers around the expenses involved
in preparing for one party. Jewels are mentioned, but the chief
expenses are for the hairdresser and the French dress stylist.
Only one of the girls, Gervasia, appears on the stage. We are
assured that the other one has spent twice as much upon her
preparation. Don Prudencio, the girls' uncle, reports that Gervasia has spent almost six thousand *reales* on this one occasion
and that it represents ten percent of her entire dowry. Her
appearance is perfection itself. Nevertheless, the two fiancés,
frightened by such lavishness, make their excuses and leave.
Gervasia asks her uncle what their departure means and what

she should do. He replies with restrained sarcasm, mixed with kindness, that she should go on to the dance as planned and hope to meet a man who appreciates her stylish qualities. Gervasia, however, suddenly acquires a convenient headache.

The same sainete has a reinforcement of the theme in a subplot at the lower level. Beltrán, a *payo*, has come to Madrid for his girl friend, Pascuala, who has been the maid in this household. He has inherited a house, stable, domestic animals; all that a peasant could hope for. When he sees how much Pascuala has changed in dress and in manner, he decides that she would be out of place back at the farm and so he returns alone.

## IV   *Mourning*

A good example of Don Ramón's satirizing of customs is the sainete that deals with the ritual of mourning. The life of a *petimetre* is a constant struggle between his nature and the artificial demands of his position. A typical *petimetre* does not feel grief but must give it the minimum observance that society demands. On the other hand, a gay party is for him a way of life, an obsession. Forced gaiety keeps him from worrying about what is happening to his country. It shields him from dark thoughts about the emptiness of his life. Therefore even while he is officially mourning, he is thinking about getting back to the party.

Public expression of grief is older than the *petimetre*. The Church demands it. The bereaved one either feels deep in his heart the urge to mourn or else thinks that it ought to be there and tries to persuade himself and his friends that he is indeed stricken with grief. The result is the rigid formula expressed by *Visita del duelo* (*The Mourning Visit*). For Ramón de la Cruz, grief should be spontaneous, unstudied, never formalized, except that probably the time established for the mourning period should be observed. The reader is perhaps not surprised to see in this sainete a group of people who want to get the formalities of mourning over with so that they can have their accustomed party. The problem is that the visiting relative is one who takes the ritual seriously. In preparing for this visit, the children are admonished about the necessity of quiet and of grave expressions. One of the guests sees to it that the clock strikes a new

hour every three minutes. The visiting relative is slow to leave
and finally the children call attention to the hidden blind musicians, eager to start the party. The visiting mourner is duly
shocked, but the hostess makes the best of a bad situation by
persuading her guest to stay for the fiesta.

Other sainetes show how short the mourning period can be.
*The Angry Chestnut Sellers*, already mentioned, has a widow
remarry seven weeks after her husband's death. *El café de
máscaras* (*Mask Wearing in the Cafe*) provides one widow with
the opportunity for socializing just twelve days after her her-
band's demise. Of course she rationalizes her conduct and tries
to convince her daughters that they should not go without masks
or otherwise reveal their identities in their outing. Such com-
punctions do not last long. In fact this play gives other persons
a chance to do things they would hesitate to do without disguises: a daughter comes to the same café that her father is
attending and almost succeeds in escaping his attention. One
lady breaks away from her husband and causes him a problem
when he thinks that another lady, similarly dressed, is his wife.
Not only are the antics of the party lovers satirized; the non-
*petimetre* upper classes are shown to be quite dour and miserly.

## V  *Curiosity and Jealousy*

One amusing sainete which has escaped the attention of most
critics is *La curiosa burlada* (*The Nosey One Tricked*). The
humor in the sainete seems quite universal, but its setting is
peculiarly Spanish. Elections are imminent and the husband
hopes to become magistrate. The real power for election is in
the hands of the marquis whose estates are nearby. Strangely
enough, the central figure of the plot of this sainete is neither
the curious woman nor her husband; it is their daughter, a girl
with three suitors: the one she wants, the choice of her father
(a man entirely too old), and the choice of her mother (a person
from the mother's village). The marquis proposes a plan which
will decide: (1) whether the wife is really too nosey, (2) whether
the husband can control his wife (if he can't, he shouldn't be
magistrate), and (3) who should marry the daughter. A package
is left in the care of the husband for one day. He is told that

under no circumstances is he to allow his wife or anyone else to open the package. When the marquis leaves, suspense begins to mount. Soon the wife is pressuring her husband to allow her to see what is in the package. She will simply take a peek and immediately put it back into place and no one will know. Soon the husband yields to this pressure. The contents, two homing pigeons, escape. The marquis now has proved that the wife is too curious, the husband too weak to seek high office, but at least the daughter gets the man she wants, the lackey of the marquis. The marquis furnishes a dowry.

A sainete not in Don Ramón's usual vein is *El sueño* (*The Dream*). Don Patricio is pathologically jealous. The servants and neighbors think of him as an extremely violent man. Don Anselmo is the only one who can talk to him without antagonizing him. Patricio has had his niece taken away to a boarding school since he thinks that Don Julián is pretending to court her openly in order to be able to aspire secretly to the favors of Patricio's wife, Ana. He considers that Ana has been cold toward him, and he has actually counted the small number of times that she has addressed him in loving terms. When she comes to him with affection, he thinks that she has some deceit in mind.

Ana talks with her maid, Frazquita, telling her of her efforts to please her husband and how they are received. She tells her of a dream that she had in which Don Julián came to see her. Her house in the dream was a medieval palace; all the servants were asleep, drunk, or interested in furthering a romantic but illicit love. In the dream Don Julián tells her that her niece, Angelita, is only the pretext for his visits, that she is the one he loves. They hear a voice and she locks Don Julián in the closet thinking she hears her husband; it turns out to be a monster.

Don Patricio, eavesdropping, hears Ana and Frazquita, and believes that he is listening to an actual experience instead of a dream, and goes wild with jealousy, trying to break down the door to the closet. The servants enter, to receive from Don Patricio the accusations attributed to them in the dream. When his wife appears he tries to get her to unlock the door. She does not have the key; he has it, but his dream-induced rage made him forget it. Meanwhile Don Julián enters through the main door along with various other people including the niece and Don Anselmo. Don Patrico suddenly sees the error of his ways

and the sainete ends happily with his approval of the marriage
of his niece to Don Julián.

The treatment afforded this subject is unusually serious for
a sainete. When Frazquita sings to Doña Ana to try to cheer her,
the words are: "For the impertinent jealousies usually pass from
imagined to true and so I doubt not that suspicion kills many."
Almost certainly, Ramón de la Cruz was thinking of the "Curious
Impertinent" episode in *Don Quixote*. Doña Ana's dream with
its ambiguous details seems to describe very plausibly the workings of a mind driven to distraction and given partial release
through the dream. The only unrealistic note is Don Patricio's
realization that his jealousy is unfounded, a happy *dénouement*
considered desirable for ending a sainete.

The *petimetre* society, as we have seen it in Cruz's sainetes,
accepts the *cortejo* as normal for its social structure. *The Dream*,
on the other hand, is more like a Golden Age honor play. Perhaps
reading between the lines, we conclude that a man must be
insane in Don Ramón's world to have the sentiment of jealousy
(*pundonor*) whether there is any justification for it or not. The
play is in the tradition of the Spanish *comedia de figurón*, developed further by Molière, of having a grotesque person for the
protagonist.

As we glance back over these sainetes of daily life, we may
wonder whether Ramón de la Cruz hoped to improve society by
his dramatic efforts. Surely he wanted to see people acting
sensibly and honestly. He hated deception, and perhaps self-
deception most of all, but it is hard to see here an intentional
crusade for human betterment. A stronger motivation for Don
Ramón's theater is the fun he gives us when we see human nature
through his eyes. The fact that Don Ramón can communicate
with us almost as well as he did with his contemporaries is evidence enough that he is telling us in his inimitable way that
fundamentally human nature does not change.

# CHAPTER 6

# *Miscellaneous Sainetes*

### I  *Satirical Sainetes*

WE noted earlier that as Ramón de la Cruz began to score
hits in his sainetes of *petimetre* society he found himself in a
literary quarrel with some of the learned men of his time such as
Nicolás Fernández de Moratín and Tomás de Iriarte. He seldom
spoke out directly against his adversaries, even to defend himself
from attack. He preferred to let his sainetes speak for themselves
and for him. In the majority of the sainetes humor was the salient
feature. To make fun of a fop or to laugh at the struggles and
machinations of a parasite is not to declare war upon them, and
any personal feeling that the author had is thoroughly sub-
merged in his creation. Nevertheless there were a few sainetes
in which the author's emotions are so strong that the sainetes
seem like ammunition in a political war and there were others
that were organized as an imitation military struggle. In such
sainetes, laughter usually gives way to anger and the urge to
criticize takes precedence over the mandate to amuse. The
sainetes which follow may or may not have been Don Ramón's
conscious effort to answer his critics, but they seem to share a
spirit different from most of the others. *The Parties of Madrid*,
considered elsewhere, belongs in spirit to this group.

In the sainete *Cómo han de ser los maridos* (*How Husbands
Are Supposed to Behave*), the idea of conflict is emphasized
from the beginning. Don Ramón, a *petimetre*, asks his lackey,
Roque, for his sword and gets angry when Roque asks where it
is. Don Ramón speaks of the poor quality of servants. Roque
replies that if Don Ramón spent as much time on books as he
did on primping he would be really learned. Don Ramón is the
*cortejo* for Doña Elena. The scene shifts to her house where her
husband, Don Pascual, rebelling against the entire social setup,
grabs a shotgun and attacks the French barber, the clothing

stylist, and a couple of others. They come running to Don Ramón
for support against the husband. Roque rather openly praises
Don Pascual, but his words are for the audience as no one on
stage takes notice of them. Don Ramón promises to straighten
things out and goes to Doña Elena's house. Don Pascual is ready
to use his gun upon Don Ramón, but other people arrive. All
criticize Don Pascual for being unwilling to allow his wife to
dress as she wishes. He asks each person connected with Doña
Elena's dressing entourage for the price of each of the goods and
services necessary to her idea of being well dressed and properly
groomed. After this substantial sum has been calculated, Don
Pascual says he will pay it, but that he wants his children to
witness what is happening to their inheritance. Two boys and
two girls appear in rags, complaining that they do not have
enough clothing and shoes to go to school. Of course Doña
Elena is now shamed to the point of mending her ways.

It is easy to see that this sainete is more melodramatic than
humorous, that its purpose is predominantly reform rather than
entertainment. It is odd that our author has used his own name
as the name of his villain. This sainete appeared at Christmas,
1772, just before the fall of the Count of Aranda, the most
powerful supporter of the enemies of Ramón de la Cruz.

The sainete most cited as politically motivated is *¿Cuál es tu
enemigo?* (*Which One Is Your Enemy?*). A sexton, a doctor,
and a fencing master are about to kill themselves because each
has a rival who is more successful than he although each rival
has had less formal training. Finally the doctor suggests that
instead of commiting suicide they might try to convince the
public that they are the true masters of their professions. They
decide to write satires, pointing out the defects in each of their
adversaries and thus achieve the respect which they think is due
them. Their rivals, however, remain more popular, and the
people seize the complainants because of their calumny. The
magistrate releases them and contests are held. The fencing
master loses to the big amateur. The doctor proves to be much
less popular and effective than the surgeon—whom the doctor
calls a barber—while one sexton who feels no envy outperforms
in verse the one who feels that he is superior. A critic who had
sided with the stuffy envious ones is brought down with them.
Who, then, is the enemy? There is no enemy. If one person is

less popular, it is probably because he is less talented, but there is no need for conflict.

Ramón de la Cruz thus pictures himself, apparently with justification, as the one who has won a contest in which the public at large is the judge, and he ridicules those who use various rationalizations to explain away what is really a defeat for the neo-Classicists.

Don Ramón's most devastating attack upon the neo-Classicists comes in the mock tragedy, *Manolo*. For once he is able to combine strong emotions with real humor. So that the reader can understand the plot from a synopsis, an explanation of the prior relationships is important. Manolo, son of Chiripa who is owner of a chestnut stand, is about to return from prison. Chiripa has married Tío Matute ("Uncle Smuggler"), a tavern keeper, and wants Manolo to marry Remilgada, Tío Matute's daughter. The play has a prologue in which the actor Chinica claims that the lives of the folk of Madrid can be subjects for tragedies just as readily as can the troubles of the ancient Greeks. After the prologue there comes a strident overture of bugles and kettle-drums, after which the curtain rises on a street scene outside Tío Matute's tavern. Mediodiente ("Half-tooth") and another *majo* are raising a disturbance while Chiripa is trying to protect things when Tío Matute arrives with his retinue, whereupon the unnamed *majo* flees. Matute makes a speech about the scandal of a theft (of one peseta) in the high-class atmosphere of his tavern whose clientele are servants of coach-owning people. Mediodiente says that obviously the one who fled is guilty. Matute wants to arrest Mediodiente anyway and the latter is defiant despite the numbers he faces, but Chiripa makes peace. Remilgada wants to replenish the red wine. Chiripa wants to make certain that it has been sufficiently watered. She says that it is still Moorish and inappropriate for Christians to drink (i.e., the wine is not baptized). Mediodiente uses erudite language in making love to Remilgada, who fails to respond in like language but puns on his name and says she is thinking of her reputation.

Cowbells announce the impending arrival of Manolo. His friend Sebastián tells of Manolo's African (prison) campaigns. Since Matute and Chiripa want Manolo and Remilgada to marry, Mediodiente is jealous, but Remilgada promises she will not marry Manolo and expresses her fear that Mediodiente is inter-

ested in La Potagera, Manolo's former love. Manolo greets
Sebastián, surprised that the latter has come down from a respected first-class burglar to a lowly matmaker. Manolo asks
about old friends, all of whom are in jails or houses of correction.
He sees his mother and asks to kiss her beautiful hand with his
dirty mouth. He tells the story of his prison life, making it
sound like a great adventure. Potagera reminds Manolo that ten
years before he had promised to marry her. He replies that he
wishes to remain free—puns on the two meanings of *esposas*
("wives" and "handcuffs"). Matute expresses willingness to com-
pensate Potagera for the loss of her honor. She places its value
at more than a hundred duros, but he offers her two pesetas.
Mediodiente, spoiling for a fight, offers to defend her honor,
almost getting into trouble with Remilgada for doing so. A general free-for-all ensues, during which much damage is done to the
chestnut stand and Manolo and Mediodiente have their private
fight. Manolo dies in his mother's arms as Mediodiente is exul-
tant and Remilgada relieved. Chiripa kills herself because her
son's death has deprived her life of meaning. Her husband kills
himself to avoid paying his wife's funeral expenses and the
expenses of mourning. Remilgada kills herself because her father
is dead. Potagera plans to kill herself for love of Manolo, but she
prefers to go to bed to die in comfort. Sebastián and Mediodiente
are left to discuss the matter. To die or not to die; that is their
question. Mediodiente decides that the more gloomy one must
live to tell of the tragedy properly and Sebastián asks Mediodiente to live to proclaim that Sebastián died of laughter.

This is a very striking parody of the vacuous neo-Classic
tragedy of eighteenth-century Spain. Every detail seems to have
been thought out to be part of the satire. The tinny overture,
the pompous arrival of Matute, Mediodiente's manner of lovemaking, and above all, the hilarious mass suicide finale, show
in caricature the low estate to which tragedy had fallen. Don
Ramón has managed to make each character true to the general
types of all of his sainetes and yet equally true to the special
needs of parodying the tragedians. Only in the mass death scene
do the *majos* have to step out of character to serve their special
burlesque function. *Manolo* was followed a generation later by a
sequel (*Manolo*, Part II) of vastly inferior quality and only
doubtfully of Cruz's authorship.

Don Ramón rubbed salt into the wounds of his enemies in 1778 with *El café estrangero* (*The Foreign Café*). The "foreigner" is named Juan Rodríguez. One of those frequenting his café is a poet, Mamerta. He is writing a sonnet and of its fourteen lines has only thirteen left to write as the sainete begins. He has written more than a hundred plays, but none has reached the stage because of the stupidity of the comedians. Each time that Mamerta appears on the stage he has composed one more line of the sonnet. This sonnet turns out to be an epitaph for a dog that was burned in a fire caused by a sigh from his mistress who suffered the terrible coincidence of having her *cortejo* leave and her hairdresser die. Before the poet can finish the sonnet, a practical joker grabs it, reads three lines aloud and "accidentally" drops it into the brazier. Also present in the cafe are a drunk who passes out, some girls who show little refinement, and a lawyer. Eventually Juan Rodríguez is arrested for pretending to be a foreigner. The reader may decide whether Cruz wants to lock up any man who is so unpatriotic as to pose as a foreigner or whether the arrest is simply a part of the parody of the *afrancesados* (French imitators).

Another sainete of this group is *El marido sofocado* (*The Suffocated Husband*). It is labeled a burlesque tragedy and assumes the form of an allegory. Juan Bueno, formerly a wealthy man, married to Lucrecia, a *petimetra*, is at the end of his rope because of his wife's extravagance. Zoilo, his lawyer, brings in an army of husbands to give advice. They counsel conformity. Two more armies arrive, an army of creditors and a force of *cortejos*. Juan Bueno makes a long speech about the sad lot of husbands and dies. Doña Lucrecia says he couldn't even die well. She must now sell a clock to be able to bury him decently. The frequent use of the word "army" and the cynical tone of the sainete suggest that here militant satire is more important than humor.

A simple little mock tragedy is *Los bandos de lavapies y la venganza del Zurdillo* (*The Lavapies Gangs and Lefty's Revenge*). Gangs from Lavapies and Barquillo Streets were enemies.[1] Zurdillo from Barquillo loved Zaina, a daughter of Tío Mandinga, a Lavapies leader. One night at a tavern Zaina had a date with Perdulario, a Lavapies shoemaker. When the time came to pay for the drinks, he said that he had no money and

asked Zaina to leave her mantilla as a pledge for the payment.
Zurdillo majestically paid the two and a half reales. Later, according to Zurdillo, thirty persons ganged up on him. Zurdillo
easily persuaded the people of Barquillo to help him with his
vengeance. He lined them up in paramilitary manner, declaring
the boys to be the infantry, the men the cavalry, and the women
the artillery. The Lavapies gang fled. Tío Mandinga was captured. His daughter made a plea for his life. Zurdillo's friend
wanted Mandinga killed, but Zurdillo decided to spare him and
Lavapies for the sake of Zaina.

This little play is a strange hybrid of the real and the burlesque tragedy, similar in this respect to *The Fritter*, already
treated. The use of low-life characters and the absurd exaggerations make it a mock tragedy. The occasional intrusion of real
emotions, on the other hand, serves to show the universality of
emotion and that Don Ramón's satire of neo-Classic drama and
his defense of the common people of Madrid often go together.

## II   *The Stage as Subject Matter for the Sainete*

From our position two hundred or more years after the appearance on the stage of the sainetes of Ramón de la Cruz, it is easy
to forget that what we now see on paper was once very much
alive on the stage and that the work of other professionals was
as important as that of the author in determining the nature of
the production and its effectiveness. We are referring to the
actors and actresses, the director, and indeed, to a very large
extent, the spectators, whose collaboration was extremely important in determining the nature and qualities of the play. Don
Ramón sometimes takes us into the world of the stage itself
when he introduces a sainete.

Interest in the inside story of the theater was stimulated by
the fact that in the popular theater of Madrid the actors and
actresses were well known to the theater goers and were looked
upon almost as personal friends by the spectators. Of course Don
Ramón did not overlook this quality of public intimacy. Frequently he would have the characters appear on stage in the
sainetes under their own names, even including them in the titles,
such as *Chinica en la aldea* (*Chinica in the Village*) and *La
hostería de Ayala* (*Ayala's Inn*). Occasionally the subject matter

for a sainete was a behind-the-scenes view of the stage in operation. The actors and actresses naturally loved this treatment. Having proved that they were skilled in portraying other personalities, they liked the opportunity of simply projecting themselves and revealing some of the formalities and informalities of their work.

The importance of the spectator can hardly be overemphasized. In France, for example, an authoritative spectator might sway opinion about a play in a way decisive to its success or failure. We can read such things as "the play was coolly received until Louis XIV saw it and laughed, when suddenly all Paris discovered its wit and charm."[2] In Spain, however, it was the common man, buying his ticket, proclaiming loudly his own taste, and arrogantly disdainful of other opinions, who determined the nature of the fare. Lope de Vega had recognized the influence of the common man in his *Arte nuevo de hacer comedias* (*New Art of Writing Plays*) in 1609. By the time of Ramón de la Cruz the effort was being made by intellectuals to impose the French style upon the Spanish theater. It had a partial and strictly artificial success during the political supremacy of the Count of Aranda. Don Ramón had to tack his sails to survive in the new wind. This period was short, however, and it was even hinted that the theater spectator engineered the eventual downfall of Aranda.

Don Ramón's technique in exploiting the goodwill among the actors is seldom better shown than in *El teatro por dentro* (*The Theater Seen from Inside*). The first scene is outside the theater where the aficionados watch while the cast shows up for preparations and rehearsals. Later we see the stage with the curtain reversed to give the illusion that it is being seen from backstage. Most of the characters simply play themselves, and a number of the biggest names in show business have merely a line or two. It is the year after the death of María Ladvenant who had been both prima donna and directress before she was twenty-five. Now the leading actress is Paula Martínez Huerta. The cast includes a very old man, José García Hugalde, and a very young girl, María Josefa Huerta, sister of the prima donna and destined to surpass her. The group naturally includes the great little comic actor, Gabriel López (Chinica) and José Espejo, who excelled at that time in parts for middle-aged men.

The plot included some theatrical criticism with the actors defending the traditional Spanish technique of mixing the comic and the tragic—acceptable and recommended so long as it remained true to life. Also defended were the "musketeers," the standing spectators who had been accused by the intellectuals of not understanding the subtleties of the theater. Most of the brief time was spent in getting the characters introduced. In addition to the ones already mentioned were: Mariana Alcázar, the second lady, Francisca Ladvenant the comedienne, and Casimira Blanca, called La Portuguesa, who for years was featured regularly in Don Ramón's sainetes. Quickly, some of the petty problems of getting ready for a play were dramatized, leaving the impression that a few were worried about whether everything was going to be ready, but most were quite casual.

*El pueblo quejoso* (*The Querulous People*) also shows most of the actors playing themselves. Here the emphasis is somewhat more that of using the sainete as a means for the actors (and naturally, Don Ramón) to criticize the type of play they are getting. It is of course another blow in the struggle between the traditionalists and the Gallophiles. Don Ramón proclaims the good taste of the common people, defends their national drama as superior to the foreign drama, and praises the actors, and especially the actresses, on the Spanish stage. A *tonadilla* (solo) provides a musical interlude which chides those who try to speak for the people instead of letting the people speak for themselves.

Don Ramón often retains his light touch even in an area in which he is emotionally involved. In *The Querulous People,* the actor Ayala enjoys himself (while other actors are discussing serious matters) by showing mock embarrassment and pretending not to know how to behave in the presence of *petimetras* after making passes at so many pretty servant girls, and also by stepping to the Prado Boulevard, presumably in contrast to those actors and actresses who seem always to get exotic and unrealistic roles in plays not by Don Ramón, and who therefore must go to distant lands.

A play devoted completely to the actors and actresses is *Soriano loco* (*Crazy Soriano*). Cristóbal Soriano, in this sainete, responds to an unusual range of acting demands. He meets various actors, each time changing speech or personality. He begins with his normal accent, but he speaks nonsense, somewhat in the manner of *Hamlet's* Ophelia. He bumps into José Espejo, who is playing the role of a blind man, and sings a duet with him. Francisco Callejo talks to him and Soriano immediately switches to a Galician dialect. Vicente Merino speaks to him. Merino is dressed as a Frenchman but has been talking in good Castilian. Nevertheless, Soriano begins to speak to him in French and Merino responds in French. Then Soriano sings a French song. Josefa Figueras and Polonia Rochel try to calm him and he waxes romantic. Mariano de la Rosa, dressed "as a Greek or Turk," thinks that Soriano's madness is feigned so that he can get amorous attention and Rosa threatens him. Soriano, then remembering *La Briseida*, one of Ramón de la Cruz's full-length plays, confuses Mariano with Agamemnon, and his madness takes the form of a martial speech. Soriano is finally calmed by the singing debut of Catalina Tordesillas, and this ends the sainete. Another person who makes his debut here is the director, Eusebio Rivera, formerly an experienced actor. All of the actors and actresses appear under their own names. It is apparent that Ramón de la Cruz enjoyed excellent rapport with the cast.

*El examen de la forestera* (*Judging the Stranger*) seems designed to introduce a new actress to the stage. She is Josefa Pineda, called la Jerezana since she is from Jerez. A lady invites two *petimetras* to meet the newcomer. A page and two maids quarrel before the guests arrive. One of the maids is for seniority privileges, the other for democracy, while the page doesn't want to sweep since it is woman's work. When the newcomer arrives, one of the maids calls attention to the fact that she also is a southerner. The maid is María de la Chica, called la Granadina because she is from Granada. Apparently many in the audience know the cast well enough to appreciate this. The group exchanges views on the differences in customs. Southerners, as depicted here, are plainer and less devious than people of Madrid. The newcomer is asked to sing a song and the sainete ends with her performance.

To explain the nature of comedy to the very audience that sees it presented on the stage sounds presumptuous. Don Ramón gets away with it by giving a sainete a fictitious audience of semiprimitives in *Los cómicos en Argel* (*The Comedians in Algiers*). A company of comedians has been captured by the Moors. They are wearing old clothes but have rich-looking costumes with them. They are brought before the Bey and his court and try to explain the nature of their profession. The Bey thinks they are from some unknown province and asks if it is an old one. The comedians, still speaking of their profession, say that it is quite ancient. One explains that he is a leading man. The activities he describes as a Don Juan annoy the Bey, so another actor, anxious to curry favor with the Bey, claims that he is not a member of the group but is a famous doctor. The Bey is delighted since he has just put to death his favorite doctor for failure to give him a method for walking a lot without moving his legs. Also, he has hanged a surgeon from a battlement because he could not remove the Bey's brains through his nostrils to wash them with soap and replace them without hurting him. One of the comedians finally says what amounts to a statement of the function of comedy. "Our direct profession is to censure the defects of men in such a way that the very censured ones will honor us, be grateful for the ridicule, and pay for seeing it exposed to the public." The Bey is anxious to see such a play. At the end of the play he is fascinated by their songs and releases them all.

To one reading *The Comedians in Algiers*, the definition of comedy's function is perhaps more significant than is the sainete itself, and is especially appropriate to the Spanish people. When we see Spaniards presenting a proud and often completely unrealistic stance before the world, we tend to forget that they do not always take themselves too seriously, and when they do not feel the pressure from outside, can laugh at themselves as well as any group can. For the sainete as acted, however, the salvation of the comedians is in song. It seems most appropriate as the best way to impress the fictitious primitive audience and end the play in a manner appealing logically to them. Looking at it from the point of view of the cast, it gives an apparently well-deserved compliment to the singers.

When one refers to the stage in Spain, one usually thinks of either the Cruz Theater or the Príncipe, both of Madrid, but Don Ramón likes occasionally to recognize the small-town drama. When a play is to be presented in the fictitious little town of Valmojado, *La comedia de Valmojado* (*The Comedy of Valmojado*), everyone from the mayor on down participates and is interested. In this case, comedians from Madrid are visiting, and so it is really a special occasion. One person remarks that Valmojado is more progressive than Madrid since there is no rule requiring a board across the floor of the stage to hide the ankles of the actresses. A debunker replies, "So what, if the girls' parts are all played by men?" The play—within-the-play—to be presented here is *The Sacrifice of Eugenia* and it is soon apparent that it is an imitation (for Ramón de la Cruz a parody) of *Iphigenia at Aulis* since it deals with a proposed sacrifice of the king's daughter to obtain a favorable wind for navigation. A few modifications of the tragedy are in order. For one thing, it is really not a tragedy since Eugenia does not have to be sacrificed but is free to marry her lover. For another, Eugenia's mother is not called Clytemnestra as in the original Greek play; her name is Achilles. There are little mishaps in the performance: the leading tenor suffers a fall, and there is a difference of opinion as to whether he should quit, remain on the floor singing, or get up and resume his aria. One of the visitors tells them not to worry since things like this occur constantly in Madrid. The father of Eugenia, who really is named Agamemnon, claims that his daughter should have shaved before kissing him on the stage. One can conclude that Don Ramón greets small-town theatrics with a mixture of derision and sympathy.

Don Ramón's interest in the theater, as a subject for itself extended even to amateur neighborhood productions. In *La comedia de maravillas* (*The Comedy of Marvels*), the play is to be presented in a rather humble private home. The word gets about quickly, and people want to get into the house long before the time for the function to begin. The cast has some difficulty getting in since the doorman has some trouble distinguishing them from spectators. A marchioness has been persuaded to attend. In order to find proper seating for her and her escort, two women have to be moved out of their chairs. One puts up considerable resistance before yielding her seat. She claims the right to one of the best seats in the house since her husband has an important role—that of the second leading lady! The house is rather dark because the number of candles is inadequate. The prompter, a *majo*, is not very skillful at organizing. The performance gets off to an uncertain start since only one person is acting his role; the others are merely asking questions or making comments. The prompter burns himself with his candle, and in the confusion that ensues, most of the cast disappears. It proves impossible to resume the show.

In another sainete already referred to, *The Payos at the Rehearsal,* the difficulty of obtaining costumes and even of pronouncing correctly the name of the protagonist are problems that plague the peasant actors. Staging the blunders of the non-professional actors is certainly an impressive way to show problems that the professionals usually manage to overcome without the spectators' being able to realize that a problem exists. These sainetes about the staging of the sainete are good propaganda for the cast and occasionally prove to be quite good as productions in themselves.

### III   *The Sainete of the Battle of the Sexes*

It seems inevitable that there should be for Don Ramón a sainete about the battle of the sexes since the theme is so common in comedy. There are a number of plays in which a group of girls conspire to make their men behave: *Las payas celosas (The Jealous Payas)* or *La víspera de san Pedro (St. Peter's Eve),* but treatment of the theme here will be limited to some sainetes whose central theme involves a formalized struggle in which men defend their rights as men or women as women. A striking example is *La república de las mujeres (The Republic of Women).* These women have retired to an island where under military rule they live as chaste as Diana herself, and their only contact with men is that they have slaves to do all of their manual labor. Chinica appears on this island as a shipwrecked fugitive and soon falls into the hands of two of the warrior women. He is doomed to death for the crime of being a free man but, since he has been taken by two of the less fanatic girls, seems to show more curiosity about their doings than fear for his life. He proposes that the girls let him feign femininity by making a skirt out of his cloak and by adjusting his hair a little. The two girls discuss their exotic life to edify him. Although this form of life is strange to Chinica and its manner of governing and requirement of celibacy are different from the customs that he had known in Madrid, he discovers that human nature has quite similar manifestations in both places.

A peace mission of males arrives, apologizes for the previous conduct of men, and suggests a truce and the return of the women to their former homes. The islanders are ready to talk terms; they impose four conditions for peace: (1) If a girl has not found a mate by the time she is fifteen, the State will provide her one; (2) Any ugly girl gets an income of three thousand ducats "to wash her face"; (3) The death penalty will be imposed for one who does not give women credit for their accomplishments; and (4) a single standard will be decreed for conjugal fidelity. The first three conditions are accepted without argument. The last is accepted although it is considered quite harsh. The warrior women are to return to their former homes on the mainland, and the sainete ends. Pale compared to *Lysistrata,* the sainete nevertheless comes out with some force for feminine rights in an essentially masculine world. Since the *petimetre* world is already oriented toward the female, one may be surprised to find Don Ramón defending women, but the rights that he is defending have little in common with *petimetre* society.

*Las mujeres defendidas* (*Women Defended*) also represents the defense of the rights of the fair sex. The ladies in a forum decide that they are badly treated by the men and should seek vengeance. The actress Mariquita Ladvenant persuades the others that the form of retaliation should be to show men that they are the cause of the very things that they complain about, and so the women dress very modestly and pretend to be interested in domestic duties such as sewing and even child care. The men come in and complain that these women are not acting very *petimetre*. Mariquita's husband comes in and complains in the same manner. Two *petimetras*, not in on the women's plot, enter with their *cortejos*. They are praised by the men. Then the women enumerate their complaints: When a girl is born, she is given to a nurse, and the parents do not get sufficiently acquainted with her even to be able to identify her. As a child, she is put into the hands of teachers of music and of dancing. She is not supposed to do any work, and so must try to trap the first marriageable male she can find. One of the men admits that all all of this is true. Thus, the sainete ends with the triumph of the women, a satire worthy of being compared—in subject matter if not in poetry—with the famous poem by another de la Cruz, Sor Juana. Presumably this was a Pyrrhic victory—although the

sainete does not imply it—since the men continued to behave as
they had done before.

Women, of course, are not always so firm in their purposes.
With Shakespeare's Hamlet, Don Ramón can say, "frailty, thy
name is woman." In *Los propósitos de las mujeres* (*The Resolu-
tions of Women*), Mariquita has decided that ladies are getting
a bad reputation. She has called the other principal ladies to her
home to ask them to agree to a reform. She sends the *cortejos* to
a separate room in her home to be entertained by her husband,
and the ladies are to resolve to become interested in domestic
things. One lady not told of the reform movement arrives late
with two *cortejos*, one of whom is very charming. Interest in him
immediately replaces interest in domestic matters. The other
*cortejos* are brought back from isolation. The husband thanks
Mariquita for relieving him of the responsibility of entertaining
men who know only how to talk to women. The party resumes
full force. A servant interrupts to tell one lady that her son has
just had an attack of epilepsy. She sends instructions to have the
maid, who knows a treatment, take care of him and advise her
if the boy comes to. She returns to her dancing. Another servant
reports that the husband of another lady has a broken leg. She
has him call the surgeon and asks her hostess not to have the
dancing last too long since her husband has this problem. The
ladies' attempt to reform society has failed.

In the battle of the sexes, the other side of the picture is shown
in *El pueblo sin mozas* (*The Girl-less Village*). This pueblo was
in a predicament since it had only one woman, the doctor's wife.
A council was held to determine whether to import some girls.
The doctor argued against the idea, claiming that his wife mis-
treats him. He shows how extravagant women are by presenting
a long list of things that women regard as indispensable, mostly
clothing and jewels. Another argued that women could be a joy
and that even at worst it was important to have them around.
The attitude of the council was made rather clear when the
doctor's wife came in and each member tried to think why she
should sit by him rather than by one of the others.

In the second scene, the women arrive. The men find these
women so repulsive that they send them away. The village remains without women except for the doctor's wife, who does not
seem displeased with having no female companionship. Inci-

dentally, to add to the sense of grotesqueness, Don Ramón asks, in the stage directions, that these female roles be played by men.

Finally, in *Los genios encontrados* (*Opposing tempers*), we have a verbal battle between a lawyer and a lady. The play opens with the quarreling between two sisters who live with their uncle. He is anxious to marry them off because their hostility to each other destroys the tranquility of his home. Petra is a misanthropist; her sister, Mónica, a girl quite willing to marry the soldier selected for her. Petra also has a suitor, Cleto, the most delicate man imaginable, quite a hypochondriac. Since presumably the sisters cannot debate a subject with civility, the author brings in a visiting lawyer to discuss with Petra the perversities of human nature. Petra argues that all men are bad; the lawyer, that women are worse. When it comes time to stop, she meekly accepts his argument and agrees to marry Cleto, leaving the audience to wonder what kind of marriage the shrew and the hypochondriac will make.

## IV   *Sainetes with Universal Themes*

Scholars study the sainetes of Ramón de la Cruz, and rightly so, because he reflects so well *lo español*, that which is profoundly Spanish. The qualities of universality are often fused in his theater with the Spanish peculiarities so that all can see how human the Spanish people are. Occasionally, Don Ramón writes a sainete in which the characters and situations are so completely universal that one is not aware of the Spanish qualities that are usually so prominent. Some of these show the influence, conscious or not, of the great French writer of comedy, Molière.[3] This can be seen especially in the sainetes which show the triumph of a pair of young lovers over an older man who tries to keep the young girl for himself. Don Ramón even adds the older woman who wants to marry a young man.

In *El viejo burlado* (*The Old Man Tricked*), a widow plans to marry her daughter to an old man. The daughter has a young lover, unknown to the mother. The maid admits the lover disguised as a lackey, and even introduces him to the widow as one who would like to work for the daughter after her marriage. The old man who is to be the groom arrives and talks to the daughter, soon realizing that she does not favor the marriage because she

loves another. By means of a bribe he learns from another servant
that the lover has been slipped into the house disguised as a
lackey. He devises a plan to expose the impostor and is successful, but he discovers that the lackey is his own son. He realizes
how ridiculous it would be for him to marry the young girl and
asks the widow to allow his son to marry her daughter. This
sainete could have served as a prototype for *El sí de las niñas*
(*When a Young Girl Consents*), the famous play by the younger
Moratín.

A similar theme is found in *La familia nueva* (*A New Set of
Servants*) with a more complex plot. A man plans to marry
his daughter to an old friend, and when he discovers that the
servants are trying to help her further her interest in a young
man, dismisses all of his servants except one who was considered
too dull to be dangerous. The servants arrange a plot with the
young lover and his servant. The two are to go to the house disguised as a maid and a nurse respectively and to claim to have
been sent by Aunt Jo, who has an informal employment agency.

Meanwhile, the old man, the father's choice, arrives, tired and
sleepy, and goes upstairs to take a nap. The father soon discovers
the plot and brings several constables to arrest the disguised
men. The discharged maid brings the news, but only seconds
ahead of the law. The disguised lover escapes, but his servant is
trapped inside. He is equal to the emergency. He whips off the
female clothes and, pretending to be the old suitor, expresses
indignation. The constables then awaken the old man, find the
feminine clothing beside his bed, and thrash him before throwing him into the street. The old man will not listen to any apologies and leaves town in a huff. The father then accepts his
daughter's choice. He turns out to be quite an acceptable young
man.

A somewhat reversed pattern is found in *El tordo hablador*
(*The Talking Thrush*). Don Mateo is a clerk who could move
up in the social scale by marrying a wealthy widow, Tiburcia.
He is far more interested in her young servant, María, whom he
woos, unknown to the widow. The other servants have heard a
thrush talking of Mateo's love for María. Tiburcia, incidentally,
has been holding a five-hundred peso dowry left for the maid by
Tiburcia's late husband. Mateo comes to make love to María,
while Tiburcia, warned by the servants, eavesdrops. Mateo man-

ages to see her in her hiding place, and in skillful Molière fashion, switches his words quickly to the widow. When she presents the servants' accusation gleaned from the thrush, he asks, "How could I possibly love an eighteen-year-old child when her mistress is a lady of good judgment of at least fifty-four?" She accepts without question his preference for mature ladies. She signs papers releasing María's dowry, thinking she is preparing for her own marriage. She learns too late that she has been deceived but gets some consolation in being able to marry Don Diego, an elderly notary.

Deceptions do not necessarily mean a deceiver. *Los viejos burlados* (*The Old Ones Tricked*) does not have a *burlador*. Two lovers had been separated when the girl was forced by her parents to marry a foreigner. Her lover also married. Many years later, each discovered that the other had been widowed and agreed, by correspondence, that they would marry and also that his son would marry her daughter at the same time to simplify problems of inheritance. The younger ones disliked this invasion of their freedom and were determined to dislike and disdain each other. The young people met. In spite of their resolves they fell in love at first sight. There was good humor in that their servants had been asked to convey their refusals diplomatically and found themselves contradicted when trying to carry out these instructions. The old couple met. In spite of their predilection they were disillusioned at first sight. Time and fantasy had tricked them. The play has no villain.

There are several other sainetes in which the older generation tries to influence the younger, with varied results. *El tío y la tía* (*The Uncle and the Aunt*) have nieces and a nephew whose plans do not fit theirs. Eventually his nephew marries her older niece and the younger girl has a soldier in tow. The older couple settle for each other.

In *La prueba feliz* (*The Fortunate Test*), Don Ramón decides that it is time to reward the older generation for its wisdom and good judgment. Leonor has two suitors, Bernardo, whom she adores, and Jacinto, the one preferred by her uncle. The uncle declares he will use persuasion but never authority in her choice of a mate. He proposes a test for fidelity. Leonor has an older sister whom she resembles greatly in appearance but who has chosen to become a nun. The proposed test is that the two suitors will be told that the sister has changed her mind about her profession and has returned home and that Leonor, faced with the loss of the dowry that she thought would be hers, had fled for refuge to a convent. The uncle tells Jacinto the news and asks him to meet the older sister to see whether he can change his affection. Leonor, with a dress and hair style appropriate for a girl recently out of a convent, is successfully disguised. Jacinto speaks warmly of her bearing and manner but declares that he can have no love but Leonor. Bernardo, given the same chance, shifts his affection easily to the "new" girl. Leonor profits from the lesson and chooses Jacinto.

The sainete is very well worked out, although of necessity the thesis is too pat. Cruz takes the edge off, however, by having an interesting palinode at the end. The maid, Isabel, says that few girls would get married if all men were tested in this way.

Another case in which an older man knows best is *El amigo de todos* (*Everybody's Friend*). Chinica exasperates his wife by always praising everyone, no matter what he says or does. Chinica's father has just died and, since he now has a good inheritance and a daughter ready to marry, he asks five hundred suitors to come. The one that pleases his wife will be accepted. A sampling of the five hundred appears one by one on the stage. The first is a wealthy man who is lavish with his money. The second is an army officer who is frugal with his. The third one is very proud of his Galician ancestors and is blunt in speech to the point of insulting everyone. The fourth has no vices because he never does anything. Chinica praises all of them and his wife rejects them. The fifth one speaks of how corrupt human nature is. Here Chinica defends human nature and rejects the suitor. He is the one that the daughter wants and has been coached to appear to be a misanthrope so that Chinica will criticize him and his wife can then accept him. Chinica claims that it is fine with him since he was tired of praising people only to have his wife reject them.

Another sainete about marriageable daughters is *El mal de la niña* (*The Girl's Illness*), adapted from Molière's *L'amour médecin* (*Love, the Doctor*). The play opens with the father weeping because his daughter is sick. He is a widower who had forty children; only one survived. Her problem is that she has no husband. The father is in no hurry to get her a husband because he would lose her and her dowry. He gets doctors who will give her cooling foods, then bleed her. If these remedies fail they will pray for her. Another doctor, however, plans to effect a cure by attacking the illness directly. He says that he hates marriage but suggests that he pretend to marry the girl in order to cure her. Of course it is the father, not the daughter who is deceived. The cure is complete.

*Chirivitas el yesero* (*Chirivitas the Plasterer*) is a sainete of pure farce. Manuela, Chirivitas' wife, and her sister meet two wandering *petimetres*. One offers Manuela a pinch of snuff and she runs off with the snuff box. The *petimetre* scarcely has time to collect his wits when he gets his "dust" back with interest as the plasterer accidentally bumps into him. At home a little later, Manuela offers her husband the pilfered snuff box, but he reasons that no one would accept the idea of his owning that expensive an item and he tells her to return it to its owner. Chirivitas then pretends to leave for the tavern but soon returns to catch the two *petimetres* making advances to his wife and proceeds to beat them with a staff that he uses in his work.

One of the most interesting of the farces is *El cochero y M. Corneta* (*The Coachman and M. Corneta*). Nicodemus, a coachman is a real "sad sack." His physical appearance and clothing are horrible. He has just been fired from his job because he caused his master to fall into some refuse when the master's girl friend was with him. He is given a letter to M. Corneta, a surgeon, and told to collect his back wages from him. He finally locates the place, sits down to rest, and soon decides he is too weak to get up. He asks first two men and later two *majas* to help him up. The men ignore him. The *majas* talk about him and one of them, who claims to be excessively tenderhearted, offers to throw a stone at him to put him out of his misery. They leave, and he gets up unassisted. M. Corneta's house has a very tall stairway, but instead of climbing it, Nicodemus persuades a servant to come down. M. Corneta soon appears and Nicodemus hands him the letter. M. Corneta reads the letter to him aloud, and, before he reaches the part about the wages due for his services, 472 reales, he is to receive in punishment for his stupidity, 472 kicks with his pants down, and also to be tossed in a blanket. The servants have trouble getting him into the blanket because, when they put him in one side, he falls out the other. A lackey comes from the former employer with a message to suspend the punishment. The play ends without any further mention of the back wages.

Another sainete of pure farce is *El maestro de la ronda* (*The Tomcat Teacher*). A young man has been a student at Alcalá but has not learned much about wooing the ladies. His father gets Juan Pulío[4] to teach him. Juan first gets him to dress in the proper *majo* manner and to affect a certain swagger. The student tries this but drops his cloak on the ground. Next he is told to expectorate in *majo* fashion. He tries it but unfortunately hits his teacher. Then they go to the house of the girl, Teresa, whom the student wishes to pay court to. To show him how, Juan Pulío says sweet words to Teresa. The girl responds very quickly. The student tries it and is rejected. He soon learns that the girl that his father had selected for him was really Juan's intended, so the apprentice must learn from the lesson and look for another girl. It is perhaps surprising that Don Ramón did not have the apprentice prove to be a very successful student and win the girl from his teacher.

Still another sainete in the same spirit is *El calderero y vecindad* (*The Tinker and his Neighbors*). The general mood is set immediately as the tinker and his wife exchange some harsh words. He reminds her that she is his fourth wife and states that he expects to bury her and four others. She retorts that that is what happens when a young girl marries an old man. Into this charged atmosphere the tinker's apprentice enters; he has had a rock fight with several neighbors and has given a good account of himself. The cause of the battle is the infernal racket that the tinkers make when they work, a noise greatly resented by the neighbors. The apprentice has hit a deaf man on his bad ear, a half-blind one on his bad eye, and has straightened out a man's crooked nose. The blows on the ear and eye have helped the victims to hear and see, but the miracles wrought by this violence have not brought gratitude. These victims enter, followed by a Basque woman, the wife of a guard, the guard himself, and a lawyer. None succeeds in getting the tinker and his crew to reduce the noise. Finally the magistrate and two constables appear. The apprentice is thrown into a well by the guard. The tinker and his crew are arrested. The sainete ends before there can be a ruling by a judge and no solution to the impasse is suggested.

*El no* (*The "No"*) is an amusing sainete with which to end this section. Paca and her brother are guardians for their niece, Laura. The brother wants her married and promises she will be married before the day is over. Paca is equally determined that Laura will not be wed. Laura loves Alejandro, but her aunt will not let him come near the home. However, the page, Roque, gets a job at Paca's house and lets Alejandro in secretly. Meanwhile, Paca has told Laura what a terrible thing love is and that if she ever has a man make love to her, she should always say "no." When Alejandro makes love to her, she dutifully says "no," but he soon learns to phrase his questions in such a way that "no" sounds very encouraging. Paca catches Alejandro, but Roque pretends to drive him away with fury. Laura swears that she said "no" to everything. When Roque leaves, a letter drops out of his pocket and Paca reads that he has just become a count with a huge income. She promptly flirts with Roque. The brother comes in with Alejandro and Laura, and Paca promises to sign the release of Laura's dowry. She then learns that the letter was only a trick.

# CHAPTER 7

# La Petra y la Juana

I have postponed a discussion of *La Petra y la Juana* to this point because I believe that it serves better than any other sainete to sum up the talent and spirit of Ramón de la Cruz. The girls in the title have the feminine equivalents for the names of St. Peter and St. John, whose days are celebrated close together in early summer. The setting is a tenement house, whose name, *Casa de tócame Roque* (*House of Utter Confusion*) serves as an alternate title for the sainete. The stage is the patio of this house, which has many apartments—the stage directions call for eleven. For practical tenement living, eleven apartments are probably not an excessive number for much of Madrid life, but for the confines of the stage, the crowding would be such as to suggest many more. This does not mean that the crowded conditions produce the conflicts. It does make them more public and therefore less dignified. It might also reveal that tempers reach the boiling point somewhat quicker under these conditions and that in questions of human relationships, the more public the bruising of one's honor, the more difficult the wound is to heal.

As the scene opens, we see that El Moreno ("Dusty") is sad because he loves Petra and cannot afford to honor her saint's day the way the landlord's nephew had honored Juana on the day of St. John—by a full orchestra serenade. He tries to appease Petra by rounding up a few acquaintances who are amateur musicians willing to serenade her, but Petra remains petulant. Her mood does not improve as Juana appears on the balcony to exchange insults with her. Jorge, the tailor, and his wife are on stage throughout, now to egg on the main characters, now to make peace between them. Moreno, in desperation, decides to pawn his watch and his best clothes to get money to hire a respectable group of professional musicians. He returns in tatters, but with money, stating that his "friend" the pawnbroker was charging only ten percent per month interest.

Meanwhile subplots are being interwoven. The most significant of these is the quarrel between the captain's widow and her servant Aquilina. From the servant's point of view, the mistress is cruel; from the point of view of the mistress, Aquilina is lazy. Furthermore, she is not good at guarding secrets; she reveals that the captain's widow had been the wife of a captain of thieves who was hanged for his crimes. She was prudent enough not to reveal it until arrangements had been made for her to change employment, but vindictive enough to assert it immediately afterwards. By this characterization Don Ramón exposes some of the cruelty and pathos that accompany a servant girl's life. She had put up with her employer's tyranny for eleven months because she feared that the alternative would be to take her back to Madrid's house of correction.

The other quarrels are sketched more briefly: a lawyer has hired a *pasiega* (mountain girl from Santander province) to wet-nurse his child. He complains that the child is undernourished; she, that she has not been paid. The other quarrel is between an invalid with a gun and an old woman with cats.

Juana, although fortunate enough to receive the serenade from the landlord's nephew, is not wise enough to devote all of her time to him. Near the end of the sainete, the nephew learns that his uncle has died and left him the house. He then discovers that Juana has been receiving the attentions of at least three other men. A prudent man, he does not vent his rage upon Juana. Instead, he decides to buy a serenade for Petra in Moreno's name to equalize things between Petra and Juana and to enable Moreno to recover his watch and clothes. He arranges for Aquilina to work for the tailors and decides to share a thousand pesos among his various tenants to enable them to rise above the miseries to which poverty has brought them. The sainete ends here.

The plot is interrupted periodically with singing either by the tailor and his wife or a group of blind singers. The little *tranches de vie*, so characteristic of the sainetes, fill this play. The purpose is to draw laughs, but as is so often the case in the sainetes, the pathos comes through also. Love, honor, and status combine to drive El Moreno to the extreme of pawning his last valuables to give Petra the ability, on a single fleeting occasion, to enjoy equality with Juana. Two special features add poignancy to the irony. The "friend" who receives the pawned items will charge "only" ten percent per month. And Juana, who receives the tribute that started the problem, is an unworthy girl who was dividing her affection among several men. The most thoroughly human character is Petra. If she truly loved El Moreno, she would not have permitted him to make his sacrifice, much less goad him into it. But Petra is a *maja;* she cannot be a *maja* and be unselfish, disdainful of rivalry and its challenges. In one respect the characterization does not seem typical. Moreno is not the usual *majo.* He shows less bluster and more pathos. It is unusual in *majo* society for the female to get the upper hand to this extent. Yet it is hard to see how Don Ramón could have executed his plot in any other way. He wishes to show, as he has on a number of occasions, how tyrannical a custom can be, and he wants to leave us with the feeling that Moreno could not have avoided the challenge presented by the serenade honoring Juana. I suspect that the reader prefers it that way. Moreno is too meek to be typical; Juana is too shameless. Their two characters offset each other; they are plausible, not stereotyped.

Still another title for this sainete is *El casero prudente (The Prudent Houseowner).* The *casero* made the mistake of spending money lavishly upon Juana, a mistake in the mores of this community since such generosity should have entitled him to Juana's undivided attention. In the denouement, as we have seen, he forgets about the wrong done to him and considers the welfare of his tenants. He discovers that almost everyone is seriously frustrated in his most worthy ambitions because of the lack of a small amount of money. He decides to give away that money to provide these people an opportunity that would otherwise be denied them. It shows the dawning in Spain of social consciousness which was to culminate in the social drama and novel that flourished a century later. Normally, Don Ramón pictures life as the candid camera might reveal it, and gives us little editorial comment.

We can remonstrate with him: "Don Ramón, you have shown us in many other sainetes how much stronger is human nature than is the power of a thousand pesos in effecting the decisions of a dozen tenants." We can imagine his reply: "My friends, this is still a sainete. I know as well as you do that the tenants of this house of 'tócame Roque' will squander this money and soon be as unhappy as before. Let me have a little fantasy for once. Let me picture a landlord for tenants to dream about. Let me show landlords what the power of love could do, if only theoretically, and let me harbor the illusion that one of these tenants was also prudent with the money he received and was able to make a finer life for himself by means of this little push."[1] This is the kind of illusion that Spain needs. If the good government of Charles III had been allowed to prevail, the illusion might have become a reality, but his successor, Charles IV, did not prove to be a *casero prudente*.

# CHAPTER 8

# *The Sainetes as Cultural Documentation*

## I *Their Importance*

WHEN a skilled writer deals realistically with his contemporary scene, it is certainly natural for those coming after him to examine his works for the light that they may throw upon the culture of that period. Where the official historian may write diplomatically about the great figures of his day and may cover up or omit matters distasteful to his patrons, the pen of the writer of comedy may be more honest and many give intuitive insight into matters not easily susceptible to a more formal treatment. If this is true, Ramón de la Cruz must have left a gold mine in his sainetes for the historical and cultural prospector to explore.

Mr. Arthur Hamilton, in his work, *A Study of Spanish Manners, 1750-1800,*[1] has made an important contribution to this topic. The task which he set for himself was to report what the sainetes had to say about Spanish customs without attempting to prove or disprove the accuracy of Don Ramón's reporting. His choice of the word "manners" was an excellent one because it allowed him to document, through the sainetes, all of the examples of exaggerated conduct of Don Ramón's world. Thus he has given them an aura of veracity, but has stopped short of labeling his reasearch as historical or sociological documentation. Hamilton's is a monograph of literary scholarship emphasizing the customs and manners found in the sainetes, and pretends to be no more.

The sainetes tell us that in Spain the times were out of their customary joint. Spaniards had been behaving in a certain way

110

for centuries. Golden Age drama—to the extent that it captures the true picture of its time—tells us what Spaniards were like. Don Ramón then tells us that the Spaniards of his day, alas, are behaving differently. It is obvious that he prefers the old ways and the old spirit. A study of the nature and extent of their deviation from Spanish norms could be important and exciting.

The usual reader of the sainetes is willing to believe that the world of Cruz's stage is an objective reproduction of the world that he saw and lived in, the same world that inspired or bemused Goya. It is necessary, of course, to discount the exaggerations inevitable in comic theater, exaggerations that caricature but do not distort beyond recognizable reality. We must also beware of hidden editorials, little pictures that slyly interpret while they depict, for Cruz's, like all reporting, comes from a personal point of view. The nature of the sainetes, however, predisposes the reader to accept their interpretation as authentic. The more one examines the sainetes, the easier it becomes to project himself into this world, anticipate the actions of the characters or be ready to accept these actions even when they surprise him, and to emerge with the feeling that he has truly communed with a large segment of the past. The highly impressionistic nature of the action helps him forget that a playwright is serving as intermediary.

Moreover, the logic of history is reassuring. The presence of a French Bourbon dynasty on the Spanish throne, the existence of so many government-founded cultural institutions copied from the French (such as the Royal Academies), the imitation of French literature by Spanish writers, the adaptation of some Spanish *tertulias* to the form of the French literary salons: all point to the thoroughness with which the French culture had penetrated Spain, and contrast sharply with the Spanish Golden Age literature, suggesting a natural clash of cultures and making plausible the *petimetre-majo* confrontation which forms the basis of so much of Don Ramón's dramatic art.

It seems reasonable to conclude that from the point of view of the literary historian, the sainetes do shed light upon the life of the times they dramatize by giving one astute writer's attitude toward this French-dominated society. This statement is a bland assertion of the obvious, but it serves as a point of departure for the thoughts presented in the second section of this chapter.

## II   *The Limitation of the Sainetes as Historical and Cultural Documentation*

After one has recognized the French influence and the veracity with which Goya and Cruz have interpreted it for us, the question remains as to whether there is any limit to this penetration or any area of Spanish life exempt from it. It can readily be seen that the *majos* themselves provided a type of resistance to the new artificialities, although a case can be made for considering the *majo* himself as a bastard child of the conflict between the new French and the traditional Spanish cultures. Were there any people who simply lived normally? What, if anything, did Don Ramón leave out of the Spanish character of his day in putting that character on the stage? Do the characters really represent all of the Spanish people or is Don Ramón writing about only a fraction of them?

We obviously have less than the total picture of life in Don Ramón's world for several reasons. In the first place, no one man's personality responds to all factors of his environment. Everyone is impressed by some phenomena and is oblivious to others. In the second place, Don Ramón was consciously selective. Since he was writing fiction and not history it was his privilege and his duty to choose things pertinent to his drama instead of seeking the objectivity to which the true historian aspires. And finally, Don Ramón was not ubiquitous or omniscient. Many factors were beyond his comprehension due to limitations imposed by geography or by his intellect.

Each reader has his own expectations as he examines the world of the sainetes. After reading about the preoccupation of the poor with drafts in the sainete-like plays of the Quinteros and after observing the obsessions of Spanish and Spanish Americans with the perils of exposure to the night air, I expected to see a concern in the sainetes for colds and cold weather. It would have been simple to exaggerate this concern by having a man wear a kerchief over his mouth, perhaps even indoors, or for him to move from the brazier to the colder parts of the room before going outside, thus avoiding temperature extremes. One of the rare references to a person's concern for drafts in the sainetes is found in the *Fireworks*, where a man expresses concern for his wife's health, humorous to the audience because it is July. Perhaps Don Ramón felt that those who really suffered from the climate did not want to be reminded of it in a theater which may have been drafty. This reference to a season is also unusual. The sainetes seldom deal with climate or weather. When the action takes place out of doors, it is difficult to determine the season of the year.

In the sainetes considerable interest and amusement but no sentimentality are shown over blind musicians. In only one sainete can I recall difficulties of the deaf and mute; Cruz has one character in *The Tinker and his Neighbors* report that these were cured by violent and humorous means. References to hunger are rare. Again, those who suffer from hunger are not the genuinely poor, but abbés and a student. The audience laughs at Doña Ana, a beggar in *Main Square*, but the laughter results from the remarkable success she shows at begging. Real deprivation and suffering form almost no part of this picture. There are two reasons why not, each sufficient in itself. First, Don Ramón wanted to amuse, not to shock. Second, it was not the custom in his century to use the theater to move men to social action.

Comparisons have occasionally been made between the sainetes of Cruz and the paintings by Goya. Some of Goya's scenes from daily life, the bullfight scenes, the *petimetre* children playing games, have no counterpart in Ramón de la Cruz. In fact, the children of the wealthy seldom hold a place in the sainetes, while children of the humbler classes are normally used only in rather incidental roles. These paintings by Goya were often done with great subtlety. It is well known that the royal family did not realize that he was lampooning them. The sainetes, on the other hand, seldom lent themselves to subtleties since the audience is generally unsophisticated. Don Ramón's purpose in the sainetes is to mock rather than to praise, so one could hardly expect to see serious literary discussions among the *petimetres*, to hear the music that they enjoy, or to reveal their higher aspirations and nobler sentiments. His longer plays do, albeit superficially, treat some of these qualities and the sainetes themselves show much of the native culture through the songs and dances of the *majas*.

A final limitation in Ramón de la Cruz as a historian is his limited field of observation. He was of course a keen observer of the everyday life of the people of Madrid and of those people, especially *payos*, who came to town from the suburbs and rural

areas. He was not a well-traveled man, however, and there is no
evidence that he kept abreast of developments elsewhere by
correspondence or by associating with cosmopolitan men. In this
respect his alienation from the salons and *tertulias* was a decided
limitation.

Madrid was probably the best single place from which to
observe Spanish life and undoubtedly gave more influence than
it received from the rest of Spain. Madrid was perhaps not entirely representative of the country. A number of Don Ramón's
sainetes were published in the early decades of the nineteenth
century in Barcelona and Valencia. Most of these were printed
without the author's name and generally seem to avoid the typical Madrid themes dealing with the life of the *petimetre* and the
*majo*. This suggests that, at least in these Eastern ports, neither
Ramón de la Cruz nor the special Madrid world that he pictured
held importance after his death and the death of that society,
but that those sainetes with more universal themes still com-
manded considerable interest. Don Ramón was not entirely
limited by this world that he helped to create for literature and
which in some measure can be said to have created him as a
writer. One might add that the Barcelona and Valencia printings
inspire considerable doubt as to how deeply the *petimetre-majo*
influence was felt in Spain outside of Madrid, even during its
heyday. It is a tribute to the artistry of Goya and Cruz that this
world is so vivid in our minds today that other parts of Spain
may have lived a life more or less in the traditional Spanish way,
scarcely aware of the rococo world in the court and capital.

In Cádiz, Ramón de la Cruz had a contemporary and rival,
Juan González de Castillo, who wrote excellent sainetes. Castillo's work also used local character types, but they fitted better
the idea that foreigners have of Spain than did the *petimetres*,
*majos*, and abbés of Don Ramón's plays. It seems reasonable to
conclude, therefore, that Spain did not suffer the French influence so strongly and universally as Don Ramón's sainetes imply.
Had the entire country suffered as deep a penetration of the
artificialities that afflicted Madrid, the recovery of the traditional
way of life in the nineteenth century would have been quite
remarkable.

# CHAPTER 9

# Don Ramón's Other Plays

THE fame of Don Ramón de la Cruz will rest almost entirely upon his sainetes. Nevertheless, to help complete our picture of the man and his literary achievement, we should examine his other works with some care. As usual, exact classifications are difficult, but a good working division is to put the plays into three groups: first, those based upon another man's work (translations and adaptations); second, those original works in which the idyllic, lyrical element is dominant; and finally, those in which humor or farce is the significant element. The first group is arranged according to the degree of modification or adaptation that Don Ramón makes in the original.

## I  Translations and Adaptations

Of Don Ramón's translations, one of the most faithful is that of Beaumarchais' *Eugénie* (*Eugenia*). Baron Hartley, a widower, plans to marry his daughter, Eugénie, to the brother of an old friend. Eugénie has been living with her aunt, Madame Murer, since the death of her mother. Mme Murer has (she thinks) married Eugénie in secret to the Count of Clarendon, but he has faked the ceremony. Clarendon is under the sway of his uncle, a duke, who has arranged another marriage for him. Clarendon is not a complete cad—his affection for Eugénie is genuine and what he has done weighs heavily upon his conscience. Toward the end of Act I, it looks as though there will be some sort of exposure as Hartley tells of Clarendon's imminent marriage. The Count manages to lie his way out of the immediate difficulty.

We learn in Act II that Eugénie's brother, Sir Charles, has taken flight because he has been insubordinate to his colonel. He is hiding in London under the name Campley. Hartley's friend, a captain, who has brought this news, has also brought word of the coming marriage of Clarendon to the daughter of the Count of Winchester. Mme Murer, in disbelief, says that the Count has made other arrangements. Hartley, not knowing of his daughter's plight, speaks with mixed derision and pity of the poor girls who suffer from Clarendon's levities. He does not connect the conversation with Eugénie's sudden illness.

In Act III, Eugénie wavers about making a full confession to her father. When he sees her so afflicted, he soon gets this confession. Her aunt takes up for her and accepts the responsibility for sponsoring the marriage. The father breaks down momentarily, and Eugénie can rejoice, but then he remembers that there is to be "another" wedding. He questions Clarendon's valet, but Hartley's words are so vague that the valet is confused, and as a result, the Baron learns or surmises that the wedding of his daughter was a false ceremony. Eugénie wants only to die; her aunt talks of vengeance.

In Act IV, Hartley talks of presenting his case before the King. Mme Murer moves toward her vengeance. Meanwhile, Clarendon has rescued Sir Charles and has told him of what is on his conscience. Soon Sir Charles discovers that the girl whom Clarendon duped was his sister. He feels that to be true to his family would be to be false to his rescuer. Clarendon is about to be ambushed by Mme Murer's servants and presented with a marry-or-die alternative, but Clarendon rejects this threat. So does Sir Charles, who finds the Count's sword for him, allowing him to battle his way to freedom. Sir Charles finds that Eugénie is innocent and swears that he will take over the vengeance, but openly, not in ambush.

In Act V, Eugénie tries to get Sir Charles to give up the vengeance. She says that she still loves Clarendon. As long as he is living she will have the strength to disdain him, but if he is dead she will not have the will power not to weep for him. Her words do not dissuade Sir Charles, but when he accosts Clarendon, Sir Charles's sword breaks. Honor will not let Sir Charles continue to seek vengeance since Clarendon refuses to take his life. Finally, Clarendon confesses his dishonorable conduct to his uncle, the Duke. He asks Hartley for forgiveness and wants to marry Eugénie properly. For a while it looks as if Eugénie is unwilling, but Mme Murer and Hartley are convinced of the genuineness of Clarendon's repentance and persuade her to accept him.

The way that Beaumarchais sets up the play, the reader might suspect that he is to witness a tragedy although the secrecies involved and the fears of the characters for the actions of their relatives lack the serious tone of tragedy. While Eugénie at first seems only a pawn in the various intrigues of the Count, she does manage eventually to acquire some individuality when she balances fear for her brother and mixed love and hatred toward her lover, and makes a reasonable plea for Sir Charles to put aside his vengeance. Beaumarchais has a cleverly ironic note, unfortunately repeated too often to be effective, when Hartley and Sir Charles show feelings of sophistication toward Clarendon's improprieties until they learn that Eugénie is the Count's victim. Beaumarchais seems unaware of how many loose ends the play has. Clarendon's other marriage is obviously to be cancelled, but there is no hint that serious consequences can result. Sir Charles's troubles with his Colonel have not been resolved. Hartley's promise to the old captain that he will give Eugénie to his brother has been forgotten. One will have to conclude that *Eugénie* is not Beaumarchais at his best.[1]

Don Ramón's translation has been remarkably faithful to the French original. Rarely does he reinforce the plot with lyricism of his own. The play seems to retain its French stamp in spite of the medium of the Spanish language. Neither the pathetic Baron Hartley nor his chivalrous son, Sir Charles, can seem like Spanish creations even when employing the Spanish tongue. The honor code is a French code. Ramón de la Cruz has performed simply and faithfully the duty of permitting the French play to be understood by Spanish-speaking audiences.

The language of the translation is, however, good Spanish. Few Gallicisms betray the French flavor. When referring to a deceased person, Don Ramón, as would any good Catholic Spaniard, adds the "may God watch over her" that is not present in the original. Inevitably there are shortcomings in the translation. For example: *Aborrezco a todo el mundo* (I hate everybody) seems weak compared to *j'ai le monde en horreur* (I hold the world in horror). These lapses are few.

An equally faithful translation is Don Ramón's rendition of Voltaire's *L'Ecossaise* (*The Scottish Girl*). Before the action of the play begins, Lord Murray, Senior, has caused the financial ruin and social disgrace of his enemy, Montrose. Montrose's daughter Lindane, for whom the play is named, is separated from her father and is reared in poverty and isolation. She knows the circumstances of her father's straits but has not seen him since she was a small child. The elder Murray dies and his son, a nobler character, inherits his father's estates and those taken from Montrose.

The action begins in the cafe and adjoining apartments of Maître Fabrice, where Lindane and her servant, Polly, are staying. Despite her obvious poverty, Lindane is recognized as having an air and a bearing suggestive of dignified nobility. She is in love with young Lord Murray despite her knowledge that his father was the cause of her father's financial ruin. Lady Ashton, also in love with Murray, intercepts a letter that Murray had written to Lindane. Since Lindane has received no word from Murray, she thinks that he no longer cares for her. Lady Ashton and Frélon, a pamphleteer whose business is selling scandal, conspire to have Lindane arrested. An extra character observing the scene, a wealthy and adventuresome merchant named Freeport, generously offers money to Lindane with no strings attached. Naturally she refuses it, but he later uses this money to bribe officials when Lindane is in custody. Montrose arrives at M. Fabrice's place, determined to avenge himself upon the young Lord Murray. He learns that a mysterious Scottish girl is there and contrives to meet her. Montrose eventually recognizes his daughter through their conversations and a picture that she has of her mother. Lindane tries to get him to leave London to avoid a confrontation with her lover. Lord Murray appears at the end of the play, however, offering apologies for the conduct of his father and a paper restoring all of Montrose's property and rights.

The Spanish translation is a faithful and quite literal rendition of Voltaire's play. Moratín is the authority for assigning the translation to Don Ramón.[2] There are two Voltairian subtleties which I presume were largely lost upon Spanish audiences. One is that Freeport is pictured as a resurgent counterpart to the decaying aristocracy. The other is that Lindane explains to Montrose, just before learning that she is his daughter, that perhaps she owes her nobility of conduct to the fact that she was deprived of the milieu of nobility during her formative years. These two items are quite overshadowed of course by Lord Murray's generous acts in restoring Montrose's rights to him. Voltaire's technical skill partly disguises the lack of any true reversal in the play.

Don Ramón did not have our modern perspective for evaluating these plays. If he had known that other offerings by Beaumarchais and Voltaire would have stood the test of time, he might have developed a more effective career as a translator. The quality of the Italian plays which he translated is even more doubtful, adding further evidence that the sure instinct which guided him in the sainete was likely to be lost when he turned from the sainete to the longer plays.

Two typical translations from the Italian were taken from originals by Apóstolo Zeno. One, which Ramón de la Cruz called a *comedia heroica,* was *Lucio Papirio,* named for the protagonist and renamed by Don Ramón *El severo dictador (The Harsh Dictator).* Zeno stresses the balance of power of the three Roman estates: ruler, patrician, and plebeian. Lucio Papirio, the dictator, had promised his daughter Papiria to General Quinto Fabio. Quinto had won a great victory over the Samnites, but in doing so had disobeyed orders not to fight. Out of pride, he sent a message to the Senate, not the Dictator, proclaiming his victory. Quinto's father, Marco, a consul, succeeded in getting him a trial by the Senate instead of summary punishment by Papirio, but the senators could not reach a decision and Quinto officially appealed to the people. Meanwhile, Papiria persuaded Quinto to confess his disobedience to the Dictator in private and try to get a reconciliation. Papirio tricked him by drawing a curtain to reveal that his humiliation was public.

The third act shows several reverses and counterreverses. Servilio, Tribune of the People, is in love with Quinto's proud sister Rutilia, and seems to have the people (and presumably the audience) in the palm of his hand. At one time the popular decision is to have Quinto killed, with honor. Papiria starts a revolution to save Quinto, but it is stopped by none other than Quinto's father, symbol of honor and justice. Servilio finally persuades Papirio to give Quinto a suspended sentence so that he can marry Papiria. Rutilia is grateful to Servilio for saving Quinto, but she is still too proud to marry a commoner and so gives her hand to the Military Tribune instead.

Cruz's translation is much longer than the original but in sub-
stance differs only in minor ways. He has Comino, the Military
Tribune, give a speech in which it is obvious that military necessity, not pride, provoked Quinto into battle. Thus it was only
after the deed that his pride caused a conflict. This speech, and
the words of the new title, *The Harsh Dictator*, break the balance
between the two proud opponents as established by Zeno, causing the audience to have sympathy for Quinto and making
Papirio unquestionably the villain. Thus, at the sacrifice of classical balance, Don Ramón achieves a certain realism as he chooses
sides for the audience.

Both in the original and in the translation a good situation for
tragedy is set up—the proud Dictator against the equally proud
General. The former represents the newly-acquired power; the
latter, the old-line family with centuries of illustrious ancestors.
There is also a good contrast between Rutilia Fabio, the proud
sister of Quinto, and Papira, the more feminine girl who wanted
harmony and did not think pride should disturb it. The authors
could not sustain their dramatic conflict well and the result is
mediocrity.

The other Zeno play, *Sesostri*, again named for the protagonist,
is labeled by Don Ramón as a tragedy, though the villain is the
only one who is killed and there is no hubris. Before the action
of the play, Amasi has murdered Aprio and seized his throne,
killing all of Aprio's sons except Sesostri, the eldest. The Queen,
Nitocri, is left at liberty for strategic reasons and Amasi pretends
to court her while he consolidates his hold on Egypt. Amasi intends to marry Artenize, daughter of Fanete, the principal Satrap.
He believes that the affection of the populace for Artenize will
insure domestic peace if she is the queen.

Sesostri, with Fanete, comes on stage after the Prince has killed
Osiri, natural son of Amasi, and thinks that he has also killed the
tutor Canopo, who accompanied him. Fanete urges Sesostri to
pretend to be Osiri and to pretend to have killed Sesostri so that
he may choose the right time and place to kill Amasi. The circumstances which make this idea plausible are that neither the
killer nor the victim has been in Egypt for fifteen years and
therefore a letter from Osiri's mother, a ring, and Sesostri's own
sword (formerly his father's) will serve as sufficient identifica-
tion. Fanete feels strongly that their need for security is such

that neither his daughter nor Sesostri's mother should know of the plans of Sesostri or be able to identify him.

The plans begin to work well as Amasi accepts Sesostri as his son Osiri, but Artenize is placed in a puzzling dilemma since she has fallen in love with Sesostri as a stranger. As Osiri, he should be the object of her hatred. The mother, Nitocri, wants to kill "Osiri" as the "murderer" of her son and she almost does. Ironically Amasi saves him. Fanete's plans seems to fall through completely as Canopo gets to Amasi with the help of Artenize who does not know the meaning of Canopo's existence. Amasi plans to have Nitocri kill her own son, but the loyal Orgonte comes in with the rebel army to save Sesostri. Sesostri prevents the rebels from profaning the temple by refusing to let them kill Amasi inside. He and Artenize are together as the play ends.

In Don Ramón's version, the play is much longer, but the changes are minor ones. When Nitocri (Nictocris in Spanish) is about to kill her son, he has a long lyrical soliloquy and she, seeing the benign expression on his face, hesitates and must renew her anger before she finally makes the attempt to kill, thwarted by the usurper. Cruz does not allow Canopo to reach the King, but in his last moments, Canopo gets a letter to Artenize who ironically passes it on to Amasi. Cruz has Sesostri(s) show clemency to Amasi(s) but the latter kills himself.

This play is no true tragedy; it is more a melodramatic tragicomedy. Sesostris as a hero is absurd, especially in the Spanish version. He slays one man and wounds another before the play's action starts. He seems to regret the need for the killing, performed only in obedience to the written will of his dead father. He shows his impatience to kill the King in Act I, but in Act III, with far greater motivation for vengeance, pardons him. At the climax of the play, he faints in his mother's arms. Amasis as a villain is much better drawn; he is consistent, resourceful, and, at times, diabolically clever.

The play, in both versions, revolves around the mental and spiritual leadership of Fanete, but he is forced into the background at the end. On one occasion, not included in the original, Don Ramón engineers a clever ploy, deceiving with the truth. Fanete promises Amasis that he will see Artenize married to the King that very night. Unfortunately a repetition of this ploy reduces its effectiveness. Don Ramón experiences difficulty in the

exposition when he finds it necessary for Fanete to rehearse
things that Sesostris already knows—so that the audience can be
told of them. Again Don Ramón has selected an uninspired
model, and, while his version is reasonably faithful to the
original, it scarcely adds luster to his fame as a dramatist.

A somewhat happier effort, perhaps because it is a musical
pastoral play, is Don Ramón's adaptation of Metastasio's *Il Re
Pastore (The Pastoral King)*. This play, according to Cotarelo,[3]
enjoyed a modest success due to the fine acting of Vicente
Merino, a feat not repeated in later stagings. Don Ramón gave it
an extra title: *No hay mudanza ni ambición donde hay verdadero
amor (Where Love Is True There Is Neither Ambition Nor In-
constancy)*. The setting is Phoenecia in the time of Alexander
the Great. The stage shows a hill, a river, a valley, and the city
of Sidon in the distance. Aminta, the shepherd, is in love with
Elisa and loves also the peaceful pastoral life. Elisa loves him in
return. Alexander the Great and a Phoenecian leader, Agenor,
are looking for Addolomino, legitimate heir to the throne, whose
father had been deposed years before by Estratin. Agenor con-
vinces Alexander that Aminta is the missing heir. Tamiris, daughter of the usurper, loves Agenor but fears that Alexander will
consider her a traitor because of her father's deeds. Disguised as
a shepherdess, she takes refuge with Elisa. Alexander informs
Aminta that the latter is the rightful heir, that the tyrant has
been deposed, and he is to reign. Aminta doubts that he has the
qualifications for leadership, but Alexander compares the duties
of a good king and a good shepherd, and so Aminta commends
himself to Heaven and accepts the kingdom. Alexander holds no
rancor toward Tamiris; in fact, he decides that if she marries the
new king, she will have the throne that she would have inherited
if Alexander had not deposed her father. This is a bitter decision
for Agenor, but he does not remonstrate and so Alexander does
not learn of his love for Tamiris. Agenor advises Aminta to rise
above his passion and accept the marriage as arranged by Alexander. The two meet their loves but do not commit themselves;
they stall through the end of the second act. In the third act,
Elisa and Tamiris come to Alexander to tell him of their loves
and Aminta appears in shepherd's garb again to plead that he be
allowed to give up his kingdom to be able to marry Elisa. Alexander decides that the two pairs of lovers should marry and
Aminta will keep the kingdom.

In Don Ramón's play Aminta is called Mirteo. He adds minor characters and a *gracioso* (comic). One interesting addition is his having Alexander decide that, since Tamiris is being deprived of her kingdom, she and Agenor will have the very next kingdom that Alexander conquers. Instrumental and vocal music add to the enjoyment of the play. Neither the plot nor the characterizations mark this play as superior to the others that we have discussed, but the fact that the setting is pastoral rather than classical makes the characterizations more appropriate.

One of the more charming of Don Ramón's longer plays is *La Espigadera* (*The Gleaner*), adapted from *Les Moissoneurs* by Favart; the ultimate source is the biblical story of Ruth. The Naomi of the biblical story is changed by Don Ramón to a kindly stepmother, Matilde, but the characterization of the two women is developed in a naively idealistic way and given an attractive Spanish setting. Don Diego is a wealthy man, very kindly disposed to those who work on his farm. Matilde and her stepdaughter Benita live near by. Benita is a sensitive, frail girl who gleans from the fields to get enough to eat. Jacinto, a city slicker, comes, pretending to be hunting. He is Diego's nephew. He has met and formed a passion for Benita, and has come to try to get her. Diego learns that Benita is his cousin and plans to have her marry Jacinto, but Jacinto has his men seize Benita, and so Diego rescues her, dismisses Jacinto and decides to marry Benita himself. Jacinto seems very ashamed of himself, vows to mend his ways and return when he can be an honor to his uncle. The stepmother Matilde had not protested in Benita's name her rights to her father's property because she wanted to avoid a family quarrel and its consequent bitterness.

Don Ramón also wrote a sequel for the play. Don Diego is awaiting a papal dispensation to marry his cousin. A new villain, Eduardo, appears, a gentleman disguised as a worker. Eduardo claims that he wishes to become a worker simply because he is without funds. Actually he hopes that his glib tongue and his youth will win Benita. Jacinto (Diego's nephew from the first play) returns. He is now interested in a girl named Isabel and he knows that she and her father, Don Carlos, plan a visit to Don Diego. Since Don Carlos is a widower, he wants his daughter to have the example and counsel of Benita and her stepmother Matilde. Jacinto recognizes the villain Eduardo and later wounds him in a fight. Eduardo, not seriously hurt, knows that he has no future with Benita and leaves. Jacinto will marry Isabel and the dispensation comes for Diego to marry Benita.

The first play suffers from the excessive sweetness of all the characters; even Jacinto undergoes a rapid and sincere repentance. It does follow quite well the spirit of the biblical story, and by transplanting the setting to the Spanish countryside, the author helps give the story an aura of reality. One seldom experiences such idealism in life, but the dignified tone of the play makes it quite acceptable as a religious fantasy.

If we look at the two plays together, it seems strange indeed that so retiring and modest a heroine as Benita could attract the passion of two such distant and unworthy persons as Jacinto and Eduardo. Since the sequel does not have the biblical story to help sustain it and the audience is never able to fear that Benita will succumb to the wiles of Eduardo, the play did not enjoy the appeal of its predecessor, and one can easily see that it was not destined for comparable success.

One normally thinks that a translation is made for the purpose of presenting a play which has been successful in its original language into a different one in order to find a wider audience. On one occasion Don Ramón translated a play by Pierre René Lemonnier so that the play could be seen at its premier (and presumably only) performance, by a Spanish-speaking audience. The gala occasion which convoked this collaboration of two dramatists was the wedding of María Luisa, second daughter of King Charles III, to Prince Leopold of Austria. The stage for this play is the home of the French Minister Plenipotentiary. Since Don Ramón was also assigned to write an *entremés* and a *fin de fiesta* for this occasion, I shall introduce the entire program at this point to give the reader a feeling for the continuity of a program. We have for this purpose an attractive printed version of the year 1767 with the French text on the left page and Don Ramón's translation on the right. An interesting little deception is discovered here since the title of the prologue, "Les dieux réunis ou la fête des muses ("The Meeting of the Gods or the Festival of the Muses") is so prominent that it obscures the title of the play itself, *Le tuteur amoreux* (*The Enamored Tutor*). The prologue is a gathering of the gods to give their blessing to the royal marriage.

In the main play, a comic opera, the tutor, Anselme, is in love with his ward, Laure, but has to leave for a while for a reason which is never explained. He is afraid of losing her during his absence, to Atys, a wealthy young suitor, so he hires old Jacinte as a sort of Celestina in residence. Jacinte immediately sees that Laure loves Atys and loathes Anselme. She decides to double-cross her master. Anselme's interests are protected for a time by his lackey, Guzmán, but Atys bribes him. Mantó, a sprite, pro-tects Atys, bringing him in disguise to Laure. Anselme returns unexpectedly. Mantó bids Atys depart, promising to protect Laure by playing upon Anselme's greed.

In Act II, Anselme plans to leave Guzmán (implausibly still trusted) to take Laure by force to a convent. Mantó causes a storm which prevents Guzmán from acting. He also builds a magic palace to make the greedy Anselme agree to give up Laure. Eventually he is made to see the folly of marrying youth with age and agrees to the Laure-Atys marriage, whereupon the palace becomes Madrid and the play's marriage and the royal one are fused in the finale.

Despite the play's shallowness and imperfections, it is sur-prisingly good for this type of made-to-order production—a trib-ute to Lemonnier's talent. The translation, a little longer than the original but facile and faithful, is a tribute to Ramón de la Cruz's capacity. Occasionally he could improve on the original: *Quel conte me fais tu?* ("What story are you making up for me?") becomes, *Con esa historia a tu abuela* ("Tell that one to your grandmother").

Don Ramón's interlude is an idyllic trifle in which gentlemen visit in the mountains of Toledo province where they find all the delights of Arcadia. There is a little Cervantine-like irony in that one gentlemen speaks of the lack of any strife among these people while the peasants do have their conflicts and worries. This little touch was probably too delicate to have penetrated the royal ears. Don Ramón also gets in a little dig at Madrid by having one gentleman say that it is easier to seduce three con-ceited girls from Madrid than the least intelligent mountain girl. At the end, two timid peasant lovers get together and decide to marry.

The sainete which serves to end this program, also by Ramón de la Cruz, is called *Las majas de Lavapies* (*The Majas from*

*Lavapies*). The scene shows the façade of the ambassador's house; a sergeant is there to prevent all from getting in. *Majos* and *petimetres* try various pretexts for getting inside. One *majo* pretends to be a hairdresser for the leading actress. Others claim to be blind singers. Finally the *majas* arrive, saying that they have a program in honor of the wedding. They are admitted by a servant of the ambassador, speaking with a French accent. Their program is centered in a flirtation between a muleteer and a tavern girl, having the aspect of a ballad. It ends in a round of praise for the newlyweds, their host, and their monarch. The two dramatic companies of Madrid were joined for this performance, which surely was worthy of the occasion that it celebrated.

Two of Don Ramón's plays are adapted from novelettes by Marmontel. The better of them is *La Amistad o el buen amigo* (*Friendship or the True Friend*). Marmontel's title was *L'amitié à l'épreuve* (*Friendship Put to the Test*). The synopsis which follows is of Don Ramón's play: From the exposition we learn that Blandfort, a British officer, and Nelson, a political figure, had been close friends at school and had remained so despite long separations caused by Blandfort's world-wide military service. While in India, Blandfort spied a young girl, Corali, weeping beside her dying father and took her to England where his mother provided her a home and English lessons. Just before he was again called abroad, his mother died, and so he left the young girl in the charge of his friend Nelson and Nelson's recently widowed sister. Nelson and the girl fall in love. He feels that his failure to control his heart is a sin against friendship and a betrayal of a special and sacred trust. Corali feels only filial affection for the departed Blandfort and her pure simple soul cannot understand the subtle workings of Nelson's sense of honor. When Blandfort returns, Nelson persuades Corali to conceal their love, but she tells Nelson that marrying Blandfort would require her to pledge her love for him, a false pledge. Nelson plans to protect his own honor by taking his life with a pistol, but Corali dissuades him by promising to marry Blandfort. She faints at the time of the signing of the marriage contract. Blandfort, noble and true friend that he is, recognizes that the two are in love and that Nelson's honor is causing this sacrifice. He insists that Nelson marry Corali and he will make her his daughter and heir.

Corali's rebellion and Nelson's pistol were Don Ramón's innovations. Otherwise his events and characterizations remained true to the original. He improved upon Marmontel's story by reducing sharply the number of repetitions of Nelson's fretting over his dilemma. The idea expressed here of the pristine purity of the noble non-European preceded Chateaubriand and the other Romantics. The test-of-friendship motif was much more plausibly drawn than in Cervantes' story of a man with an impertinent curiosity. The play is of course too saccharine for present-day tastes but can be regarded as one of Don Ramón's happier efforts in full-length comedy.

*El divorcio feliz* (*The Fortunate Separation*) was adapted to the stage from Marmontel's story by the same name. Again we synopsize the play. Matilde and her husband had a marriage arranged by others. She is bored with married life. Her husband is a tepid lover and she feels that others are enjoying life and youth while she is doing little or nothing. He is quite wealthy and also idealistic. When he notices that she is unhappy, he suggests a trial separation. She will have her own home, possessions, and servants. She accepts the arrangement, seeking happiness in a series of *cortejos*. One is insanely jealous and possessive, others are too self-centered. Each *cortejo* brings her a new disillusionment and gradually she sees virtue in her husband. To break the separation she has her husband's trusted servant replace her portrait which looked so young, gay, and cheerful with a more recent one which shows her strain, suffering, and tears. When the husband sees the portrait, he realizes that she is still unhappy and they have a tender reconciliation. The separation was a fortunate one because it enabled her to find love by returning to her husband.

There are no important differences between the novelette and the play. The character lines are a little finer in the French original. There, the Marquis was so slow in lovemaking because he felt that the Marchioness was too young. Marmontel describes in the Count de Lisère a perfect courtier who nevertheless is not a perfect lover for the young girl. Ramón de la Cruz makes him seem simply inept, lacking in *savoir faire*. The play is well structured and the moral is well presented, but the characters seem conventional and Cruz's result is dullness. It is perhaps significant that, of the two plays taken from Marmontel, the better is the one dealing with English characters, the other with French characters. Don Ramón can evidently handle a Frenchman's Englishman better than a Frenchman's Frenchman.

The play that Ramón de la Cruz apparently felt was his best was a zarzuela, *La Briseida* (*The Story of Briseis*), which follows with some fidelity the story from the *Iliad*. The scene opens with a war council occasioned by a severe plague in the Greek camp. The sage, Calchas, tells Agamemnon that the Greeks' troubles were the manifestation of the wrath of the gods over his kidnapping of Chryseis, daughter of Apollo's priest. He must return her to appease the gods. The man who has sacrificed his daughter for a favorable wind readily gives up Chryseis but demands from Achilles the release of Briseis to him. From the girls' point of view, this is terrible since Briseis loves Achilles and feels that in him she has recompense for the deaths of her father, three brothers, and her husband. Chryseis found nothing lovable about Agamemnon. Achilles allows Agamemnon to have Briseis but withdraws from the conflict. Without Achilles, Greek fortunes subside. Agamemnon is persuaded to give up Briseis and offer other gifts to Achilles but the latter refuses to be moved. Patroclus, his friend, fails to persuade him to renew the conflict, but borrows his armor. Briseis makes a personal appearance to Achilles, humiliating herself by offering to become slave to whoever will become Achilles' wife, but her plea is insufficient to get him to rejoin the Greek forces. He does change his mind, however, when his armor is restored to him, along with the news that Patroclus has died while trying to use it against the Trojan leader.

It must be admitted that Ramón de la Cruz retained a considerable measure of Homeric realism as love is subordinated, both to military necessity and to the vicissitudes of the Greek soldier's petulant sense of honor. The zarzuela is short and the action moves toward its denouement steadily. There are no subplots. The author tries to recapture the essential qualities of Agamemnon and Achilles. He endows Patroclus with a good subhero quality.

Don Ramón's basic mistake was to try to center the action in Briseis instead of in the two Greek leaders. Her love for Achilles was complete. She had completely lost a sense of pride and she consequently loses the respect of the reader or spectator. With such characteristics, her role should have been removed from the center. The climax concerns only Achilles and Patroclus, but the title and the rest of the play could have been altered to advantage to give proper emphasis to it. The role of Achilles is extremely difficult for the author to recreate, especially in view of the brevity of the drama. It needs to be built around the stubborn individualism of the Greek warrior. In a play it is difficult to portray this sulker as the very strong character that Homer makes him. Ramón de la Cruz provides the correct motions, but he cannot endow the character with real strength.

The music of the zarzuela is minimized and handled in a way which does not disturb the progress of the dramatic action. Because Don Ramón has remained faithful to the form of French Classical tragedy and to the Homeric story, he has achieved one of the better Spanish neo-Classic efforts, even if he has not given Homeric qualities to his characters, but it must be acknowledged that his competition in this area of Spanish drama was not keen.

Two of the Cruz's sainetes can best be dealt with here since they are adaptations from the French. The first of these is *El pleito del pastor* (*The Shepherd's Lawsuit*). The shepherd, obviously a rascal, has been killing sheep and selling the meat to a butcher. He hires a lawyer who tells him to say nothing but to bleat like a sheep. He does as required. The lawyer says it is the result of the beating his master has given him. When the shepherd is freed, the lawyer asks for his pay, but the wily shepherd merely bleats. The master hears about this and forgives the servant because he has done so well in tricking the lawyer. The shepherd then promises to satisfy his master by turning over the money to him.

The story is taken from the third act of the French farce, *Maître Pathelin*. Don Ramón has added the explanation that the master's beating the servant has caused the bleating and having the master forgive the servant when the lawyer gets duped. He also adds the part about the shepherd's promise to repay the master. Perhaps the changes were a concession to Spanish moral standards. It is quite conceivable that Don Ramón did not have the original text and simply knew the gist of the story. He does, however, in another sainete, *El mercader vendido* (*The Merchant Sold*, i.e. Betrayed), use the ploy of having the deceiver invite the duped merchant to his home, allegedly to pay him for goods and to enjoy refreshment, also found in *Maître Pathelin*.

Many elements of the original farce, such as having the merchant so angry with the lawyer about the cloth that he forgets about the sheep, thus completely confusing the judge, are left out in Cruz's version.

The other sainete, *Las preciosas ridículas* (*Affectation Made Ridiculous*), is adapted from Molière's *Les précieuses ridicules*. Frazco and Perico, two servants, speak of the plans of their masters for getting married. One no longer intends to serve if his master marries, but the other approves of the idea of the marriage. The masters appear, Jacinto and Roque. Jacinto is scandalized at the conduct of the girls they were intending to marry. Roque is philosophical and even amused and suggests to Jacinto a humorous revenge involving their servants. They are interrupted by Bernardo, the father and uncle of the two girls. The men take leave of him with icy politeness, and he calls the girls to discover what is wrong. His daughter explains that the men proposed marriage in a businesslike way. The girls wanted to play the game of love, to enjoy having their reputations grow in the best places, and generally to have a romantic courtship. Her cousin adds that the men were badly dressed. These girls have just come to Madrid from Segovia and are anxious to behave as they believe that Madrid *petimetras* do. When Bernardo calls them by their names, Clara and Lucía, they object and want names taken from pastoral literature. Bernardo answers that the suitors are wealthy and offers the girls the choice for the very next day: marriage or the convent. Jacinto's lackey enters dressed elaborately and calling himself a marquis. He speaks in the flowery language that they expect and wants to hire musicians to provide dance music. Roque's lackey comes in pretending to be an army officer just returned from the wars, a close friend of the marquis. The girls are tremendously impressed. The masters of the lackeys now enter with four men who strip the lackeys of their fine clothing. The daughter and niece are properly abashed and promise to follow their father and uncle's advice in the future.

In all essentials of the plot, Ramón de la Cruz has followed Molière. He has rather cleverly worked the transfer of the setting from Paris to Madrid, along with the changes in details made necessary by the changes in locale and the passing of a century. He has used verse instead of prose. He has shortened the play to get it within the time limits of a sainete. In this respect alone it is unfortunate that he has converted the play into a sainete, for Molière, in a play still quite short, was able to give full development to the role of the lackey pretending to be a marquis, but Don Ramón had to develop his character with greater haste. Admirers of Molière will especially regret not hearing the poem which the lackey recites and in which, emphasizing almost every syllable, he gives outrageous praise for the most banal linguistic constructions.

In one way Don Ramón has made a slight improvement upon the original. He established a balance between the two bourgeois gentlemen, one indignant, the other a person of good humor. The indignant one was not the one who proposed the trick. Molière had the more indignant one as the vengeance seeker, and so the other was reduced to being a companion. While Don Ramón was not able to bring out the full Molière flavor, he did produce a clever adaptation and proved that, whether in originals or borrowings, his satire is far superior to his creative fantasy for plot or characterization.

Ramón de la Cruz wrote parodies of two French plays: *Inesilla la de Pinto* (*Little Agnes of Pinto*) and *Zara*. In the former, probably based on Houdart de la Motte's story, *Inés de Castro* (*Agnes de Castro*), the magistrate of Pinto receives the ambassador of the magistrate of Vallecas,[4] proposing that the Vallecas magistrate's daughter marry the son of the magistrate of Pinto. The idea is accepted. Hermenegildo the son, however, has loved and has had four children by Inesilla, his father's maid. The boy fell in love while watching her peel eggplant. She resisted all regular seductive efforts but gave in when he threatened to commit suicide. He promised to protect her at all costs, even against a squadron of armed mothers-in-law. His father told him that he had to marry another, but he refused. His mother learned about Inesilla. Inesilla's children are brought out to evoke sympathy, and the father worries about his duty as a magistrate and as a father. He forgives his son. Inesilla faints. She is thought dead, but a bottle of sweet cordial restores her and permits a happy ending.

De la Motte's *Inés de Castro*, if it is indeed the model,[5] lends itself quite well to parody because of the melodramatic quality of the "tearjerker." It required no special skill to give it a setting near Madrid, a lower-class cast of characters, and a few exaggerations. The parody seems to have been received with some favor.

The other play, *Zara*, listed as a "new tragedy in less than one act," is a parody of Voltaire's *Zaire*. A discussion of *Zaire* would be irrelevant here since it is not necessary to an understanding of *Zara*. Zara, like Zaire, is a Turkish girl in love with a potential rival of the Sultan. The angry Sultan is ready to kill, but the prompter moves on stage to tell him he must wait until the end of the act. Later he is again ready to kill and again the prompter interposes. The Sultan then kills the prompter. This killing finishes the play in less than one act and adds little to the fame of Ramón de la Cruz.

These two examples of parodies of particular plays do not show the ingenuity of some of the better sainetes. Probably it seemed too easy to Don Ramón and he consequently did not work very hard on them. The brilliant example of *Manolo*, a parody on the general form of Classic tragedy, shows that he was capable of excellent parody when he had the inspiration.

## II   *Translations Not Certainly of Cruz's Authorship.*

There are several plays presumed to be translations for which I have not been able to find originals. For general interest and for what light they may be able to cast upon our author, I present them at this point. The most significant of these is *Bayaceto* (*Bajazet*). Since the play was understood to be taken from Racine's play, I looked forward with interest to Don Ramón's version. *Bajazet* hardly shows Racine at his best, but enough of the genius of the master of French Classical tragedy comes through to present a real challenge to a translator: the conflict of love and power, the well-motivated characterizations, the compact plot, the sense of great movements off stage, the superb Alexandrines. There is a striking resemblance in *Bajazet* to *Macbeth* in that a strong woman's ambitions, using a weaker man's actions, lead to a tragic downfall. Instead of a treat, I was presented a puzzle. Ramón de la Cruz did not use Racine's play. Either he adapted someone else's play or he created his own.[6] The only similarities between the two plays are in the title and the Turkish setting.

In Cruz's play, Tamerlán, Tartar Emperor, has replaced Bayaceto, the Turkish monarch, as the real power in the East.

Tamerlán kills Bayaceto's wife and son with Bayaceto watching helplessly. Tamerlán plans to humiliate Bayaceto further by marrying his daughter, Asteria. This plan adversely affects two other people: Andrónico, a Greek Prince, betrothed to Asteria, and Erminia, Queen of Trapisonada who has been Tamerlán's fiancée. Bayaceto shows a defiant spirit but is pathetic rather than grand. Andrónico is an appeaser who hopes that if he plays for time Heaven will tell him what to do. In the face of adversity, Asteria, hopeful of vengeance, accepts Tamerlán's demand, to the despair of her lover and the fury of her father. Erminia decides to suppress her anger and await events. Asteria regains her father's faith by a symbolic act of defiling the throne, stabbing it repeatedly with a dagger in the presence of the entire court. Tamerlán imprisons her but sends Andrónico to try to get her to change her mind and be forgiven. Andrónico, a tardy hero, makes public his love for Asteria. Tamerlán announces the restoration of Erminia to his favor and starts the humiliation of Asteria by making her his cup bearer. Bayaceto had given Asteria some poison for suicidal purposes, but Asteria puts it into Tamerlán's cup. Erminia sees her and warns Tamerlán, who promises to drink if Asteria will give half to her father or to her lover first; thus he sees the truth revealed in her face. Meanwhile Bayaceto has poisoned himself. As he dies in what he considers a triumph, Erminia claims custody of Asteria and Andrónico and sets them free to go to Greece. Tamerlán accepts Erminia's decision and declares that he no longer hates Bayaceto, and that peace and good will will reign.

The ending seems quite natural for Ramón de la Cruz. He is not interested in *hubris* so much as he is in having the play end comfortably. He never seems to be able to show fate in an inevitable concatenation of events, and apparently fails to realize that a dignified death does not guarantee a tragic figure. With all of its shortcomings, *Bajazet* is not without interest. It is probable that with a change of name the play would have seemed a more worthy creation, for then it would not have to suffer comparison with Racine's *Bajazet*.

Another play for whch Ramón de la Cruz provided a Spanish version is *La Talestris, Reina de Egypto* (*Talestris, Queen of Egypt*), attributed to Metastasio.[7] Before the action of the play begins, Farnaspes has usurped the Egyptian throne from Tea-

genes. Talestris, wife of Teagenes, worries about their son
Lagides, inasmuch as Asbite, ambassador of the Scythians, wants
to bring Lagides back with him if Teagenes is dead as is reported. (The Scythians wish to be avenged for certain actions of
Teagenes.) Teagenes, alive, counts upon the loyalty of Nealces,
prince of Tyre, and Fenicia, his beloved, cousin of Talestris.
Teagenes, disguised as Idaspes, ambassador from Syria, tries to
rescue his son, but his army is too small. He fails to convince
Farnaspes that he is really Teagenes and so his offer, to go with
him to Scythia, is not accepted. Nealces eventually undertakes a
counterrevolution which deposes Farnaspes and restores Teagenes. They decide to offer Farnaspes to Asbite, who cannot now
expect to take any other prisoner with him.

A considerable part of the melodrama is concerned with unsuccessful attempts at self-sacrifice: Talestris' efforts to save her son
at any sacrifice to herself except the one offered—marriage to
Farnaspes, Lagides' efforts to give his life for his parents, and
Teagenes' efforts to save his son and wife by sacrificing himself.
Another ploy was to have Nealces deny that Teagenes, disguised
as Idaspes, was really Teagenes until the countercoup could be
effected. Since we have labeled this play a melodrama, perhaps
we have described it sufficiently. It strongly resembles Cruz's
other plays translated from the Italian.

La Indiana (The Girl from India) is listed by Cotarelo as an
imitation of Nicholas Chamfort's La Jeune Indienne (The Young
Indian Girl). Sr. Cotarelo is mistaken here. The setting, theme,
and plot could hardly be more different.[8] Calé, a member of the
priestly caste of Brachma (Brahma), decides to burn himself to
death because his wife has just died, and he wishes to respect
custom. Azora's husband has just died also, and she is trying to
become resigned to sacrificing herself, knowing that if she does
not, she will be ostracized. Araspe, a Persian slave, tries to persuade her to live and suggests that a marriage between the
widower and the widow would solve a problem for both. Azora
proposes this to Calé, but he accuses her of wickedness for even
thinking of it and is determined to sacrifice himself. Araspe later
talks to him of the beauty and charm of Azora. He, as a slave,
had seen her unveiled. He tells his master that it is arrogant
pride, not love for the memory of his late wife, who in fact was
a shrew, that caused him to want this death. Azora returns to

ask Calé to forgive her former conduct. He sees her in the new light of Araspe's words and in her religious, penitent mood and begins to change his mind. Soon they, along with the other worshipers, are dancing, and the word seems to come from the Great Mogol that marriage, not sacrifice, is called for.

I do not know whether this play is a Cruz original. Don Ramón usually has a literary source for his exotic offerings. Perhaps he really thought—mistakenly—that the practice of the Suttee Rite extended to the widower; perhaps he was simply using a borrowed idea. This play, which represents a victory of the spirit of life over that of Brahma, may have been quite acceptable exoticism in Madrid. Otherwise it does not have a great deal to offer.

I have not located the original for the play *El fénix de los hijos* (*The Phoenix of Sons*). This play was taken from the German, presumably through a French translation. Geromo and Colasa are very proud of their son, a military officer sometimes referred to as a captain, sometimes as a major. They have not seen him for a number of years, but he writes them letters which Patricio, the school teacher, reads to the illiterate parents. Patricio starts to read a glowing letter from the son, Carlos, but he is interrupted by the news that a sergeant is trying to conscript Valentín, son of a widow, Bastiana, and betrothed to Geromo's daughter, Cecilia. The cynical sergeant asks thirty escudos as the price for not taking Valentín. Patricio finishes by reading the letter to himself and learns that Carlos will be there that day. Carlos arrives, discovers that the sergeant is not carrying out his orders properly, and has him arrested. He invites his parents to come and live on his estates, but they prefer their native village.

This is an idealized story of a man who has risen above the station of his parents, but who preserves both love and respect for them. It blends well with Don Ramón's other plays and suggests that he felt at ease in translating or adapting it. Neither this nor any of the other unconfirmed translations is a masterpiece; therefore, whether or not originals can be found for them, the overall opinion of Ramón de la Cruz as a dramatist is not likely to change radically.

### III   *Zarzuelas and Pastoral Plays*

The Ramón de la Cruz of the pastoral plays and zarzuelas seems to be an entirely different person from the one who writes sainetes. As is true of some of the translations and adaptations already observed, the pastoral originals are escape literature, moving into a world where life is always noble and hearts pure and faithful. On rare occasions there is a true villain, but more often, strange circumstances and accidental misunderstandings provide the plot complications. The most idealistic of the pastorals is *El extranjero (The Foreigner)*, which is called a comedy with music rather than a zarzuela.

The Foreigner, Rudolfo, is visiting Alberto, a Leonese bachelor. In the household are his sister Leonor, a young widow, and Pasquala, sister of Leonor's late husband. The husband had gone to the New World but was killed by a robber. Both Rudolfo and Alberto are timid in affairs of the heart and are therefore more pastoral than chivalresque. The Foreigner is in love with Leonor but thinks it all too presumptuous to let her know. He had fallen in love first with her picture. The exposition of the play is simple and leisurely since music and the pastoral setting are predominant. At length Rudolfo dares to disclose his feelings, stating that he loved the girl of the portrait. Leonor recognizes the portrait as one her husband carried and immediately faints, since she assumes that Rudolfo is his assassin. Pasquala rushes to her aid, but she, too, sees the picture, forms the same conclusion, and likewise faints. Since several other guests are present, Alberto directs servants to care for the two girls and asks them not to mention the faintings.

Alberto, speaking with Rudolfo offstage, apparently clears up the problem. Rudolfo had brought the picture and a golden pomander that accompanied it. Later, however, a letter arrives warning Alberto that a man answering Rudolfo's description and known to be the assassin of Leonor's husband had taken flight in the same ship that Rudolfo had taken. While Alberto is taking steps to apprehend him, Leonor grabs a pistol, confronts Rudolfo, and accuses him. She decides, however, not to use the pistol and bids Rudolfo leave. He declares his innocence and refuses to flee. Fortunately a second letter arrives, announcing that the criminal has been apprehended in Lisbon and that he has confessed to murdering the husband and robbing him of the portrait and pomander which he then took to the place where Rudolfo had purchased them. The criminal likewise is named Rudolfo. The two bashful men now proclaim their loves and the story ends happily. Fearing that the moral may escape the spectator or reader, the author, first in a preamble and again in Alberto's last speech, points out that innocence and truth are always rewarded.

The Foreigner turns out to be Portuguese and seems to fit well the stereotype of the dreamily romantic Portuguese gentleman. If the reader thinks that it is unusual for a man to fall in love with a girl's portrait, he can be reminded that another Celtic nobleman, Mark of Cornwall, fell in love with a strand of hair and sent his nephew Tristan to seek Isolde.

The best of the pastoral plays is *Las segadoras* (*The Harvesting Girls*), an original zarzuela with music composed by Antonio Rodríguez de Hita, who had worked with Don Ramón in *The Story of Briseis*. The première was September 3, 1768 at the Príncipe Theater, the cast of the Cruz Theater joining that of the Príncipe for this zarzuela.[9] There were two acts and a variety of meters, much of it sung. This was the first zarzuela to introduce the popular, contemporary element into Spain.

The harvesters come to work in the fields of a wealthy, relatively young widower, Don Manuel. Mari Pelaya, daughter of the old foreman, is ambitious and tries vainly to place herself in a position where Don Manuel will pay attention to her. He is a very fine man to work for, and all the harvesters like him, but Cecilia is the one whom he prefers. Perico, a peasant, also loves Cecilia and has an agreement with her brother, Santiago, that she will marry him. A letter from Santiago's father, left when he died, declares Cecilia to be, not his daughter, but the daughter of a nobleman. This facilitates having Don Manuel and Cecilia marry; Perico and Mari Pelaya form a new team.

Don Ramón's idealism, showing such a harmonious relationship between upper and lower classes, appears fully here and reminds us of his *The Gleaners*. The plot and characterizations are of course quite shallow but in good taste, and assuming that the music was good, the atmosphere seems quite acceptable.

In general terms, *Las labradoras de Murcia* (*The Farm Girls of Murcia*) is similar. The setting is a large farm near the city of

Murcia devoted to the cultivation of the silkworm. Vicente is
a member of the nobility in disguise, working as a superintend-
ent of the estates of Doña Nicolasa, a widow who is still young
but not nearly so young as she would like potential suitors to
believe. Vicente's daughter, Teresa, is loved by many, but her
thoughts are for Don Narciso, a gentleman from Valencia and a
man of mystery. The widow's son, Leandro, is a spoiled brat who
has been to the university and likes to display his knowledge,
although it always comes out as pedantic nonsense. Doña Nicolasa disdains the attentions of a merchant from Murcia, but
would like very much to marry a titled nobleman and asks
Vicente if he knows of any among the workers who may be a
nobleman in disguise. Vicente himself seems very nervous at this
news, leaving the audience to suspect that he would like to be a
candidate for the lady's hand. Nicolasa hears about Narciso and
pretends to be twenty-four, hoping to interest him. Her son is
twenty, but she decides he could be passed off temporarily as a
nephew.

Meanwhile the girls are working in the mulberry trees. Olalla,
a farm girl overshadowed by Teresa, receives some attention
from a simpleton, Pencho. Pencho's friend, Antolín, seems interested in girls as girls, but Pencho is interested in marriage and
financial advancement—apparently to avoid hard work. At the
end of Act I a storm threatens, but just as all are fearful, the
storm goes away; the lands are safe.

Narciso reports that in Valencia Don Vicente, through Narciso's efforts, has been cleared of a charge of murder. The
murdered man, a cousin of Narciso, had been interested in
Teresa and had been moved to violence toward Narciso through
jealousy. Narciso killed him in self-defense. This report opens
the way for Narciso and Teresa to marry, since Vicente has recovered his estates and his good name. Pencho and Olalla will
also marry and will serve Narciso and Teresa. The author resists
the temptation to have Vicente marry the widow. The audience
is convinced that she is not worthy of him.

It is probably clearer to us than to Don Ramón that the plot
really has little to do with the farm girls; in general our interest
in the play is in the daily life of the silk farm, the danger of
storm, and the frolicking. One special feature of several of Don
Ramón's zarzuelas is the mixture of the social classes, not as a

hint of the basic equality of the human race, but as a realistic acknowledgment of the economic plight of some of the upper class in Spain, men who have no income and must abandon any pretense to superiority in order to be able to do manual labor.

*Clementina* (*Clementine*), a musical comedy, is one of the strangest of Don Ramón's original plays. Clementina is supposedly the elder daughter of Don Clemente, a widower. Clemente's teen-age daughter Narcisa, and Damiana, a governess, complete the household. An illustrious suitor, El Marqués, a long-time friend of Don Clemente, asks him for one of his daughters. He will accept Narciso but prefers Clementina, mostly because Narcisa is still an adolescent. Clemente tells him to wait a while since Clementina has shown interest in the cloister and Narcisa is too young. The Marquis suspects the excuses of Clemente and informs the audience that Clemente, at seventeen, had married a woman of forty. In the shadow of the Marquis is Don Urbino, who makes love to Clementina, but only with his eyes. She requites his love in the same manner. He gives her some sheet music. A letter drops from it which she tries to pick up unobserved, but Narcisa has been watching her and asks to see the letter. Clementina refuses, and Narcisa later tells her father about the letter. Clemente calls Clementina and asks her about her love for Urbino. When she admits that she loves him, Clemente decides that he must identify her family background. Clementina's mother, while pregnant with Clementina, was on a journey. She and her servants were killed by thieves. Don Clemente happened to pass by, saw the bodies and saved the baby. Since his wife was so old, he decided to adopt the baby. Almost miraculously, his wife did have a baby three years later—Narcisa. The letter, which was assumed to have been a love note from Urbino to Clementina, is a letter from Urbino's father telling of her identity. So Clementina is not Narcisa's sister; she is Urbino's. The Marquis then asks Urbino for his sister's hand, but he decides that such a question should be decided by his father and by Clementina herself. He seems pleased that Clementina is his sister. The play ends indecisively.

There are some interesting features of this play. The realistic Marquis is presented with vigor and consistency to contrast with the idealistic and vacillating Clemente and the timid Urbino. Narciso is a good characterization of an adolescent younger

sister. The author did as well as he could with the rather passive
role of Clementina. Unfortunately, the grotesque elements of the
play attract more attention. The marriage of a seventeen-year-old
boy to a woman past forty seems out of place in Spain, especially
when presented in such an idealistic manner. The idea of the
pregnant woman's travelling about Spain near the time of her
delivery—simply because she liked to travel—added to the idea
of a baby's surviving inside the body of her murdered and
abandoned mother is not quite believable. The inconclusiveness
of the ending hardly satisfies the drama lover.

Three other plays can be recalled briefly to round out our
picture of this type of drama. The first of these is *Los Zagales de
Genil* (*The Shepherds of the River Genil*). Laureano is in love
with Narcisa and Antero is in love with Pasquala. Their loves are
requited, but the villain Ginés sows seeds of discord and causes
the lovers to quarrel. At length, when by chance Laureano is
talking with Pasquala, they are able to communicate to each
other that Ginés is the cause of the estrangement of the two
couples. Ginés is given a beating and the lovers get back together. What literary values there are in this play must be found
in the poetic expressions which are by no means comparable to
those of the best lyric poets of the age such as Meléndez Valdés.

*El día de campo* (*A Day in the Country*) is a plotless trifle so
completely devoid of a story that its staging and publication can
only be pathetic evidence of the state of the theater in the
1780's. A man with two nieces, accompanied by their boyfriends,
goes to the country to spend the day. They are joined by three
other men from the city and by three *paya* sisters. Their day is
generally pleasant with music and dancing interspersed with
little quarrels to add a touch of realism. One of the young *petimetras* dresses as a *maja,* an idea which seems appropriate
enough for sportswear but which embarrasses and annoys her
boyfriend. It is presumably symbolic of her protest against the
restrictions of *petimetre* life. To add to the festive occasion, the
author gives a pristine quality to the *paya* girls and to their
*payos,* who appear near the end of the play to express their
jealousy. This play was presented at the home of Don Ramón's
patroness, the Countess-Duchess of Benavente. It may be classified more as a pageant than a comedy.

*La fuerza de la lealtad* (*The Force of Loyalty*) is a one-act

musical comedy apparently timed to celebrate the ascension of
Charles IV to the throne. It features a dream scene in which
Ceres and Terpsichore descend, a prop man's triumph. One
character is a man whose loyalty to his king is stated so naively
that it almost suggests parody. Finally it has a Portuguese
gentleman who disguises himself as a gardener to make love to
the heroine. It too is more of a pageant than a comedy.

## IV  *Farces*

Our third group is a pair of light farces. These seem to be a
link between the realistic sainetes and the various idealistic
plays. The one which seems more like comedy is *El maestro de
la niña* (*The Young Girl's Teacher*). Don Roque, an abbé, has
managed through skillful flattery to ingratiate himself with Doña
Luisa, a wealthy widow. His objective is the person and dowry
of Cecelia, Doña Luisa's sixteen-year-old daughter, who loves her
twenty-year-old cousin, Silverio. Don Roque not only serves as
tutor to the girl, but begins to run the household, ordering the
servants about and dismissing the guests. Cecelia, meanwhile,
has dissimulated her scorn for the man, waiting for him to make
a slip. He finally does. He writes her a love letter which includes
remarks about what a fool Cecelia's mother is and how much
power he has over her. Cecelia, acting coyly always, shows the
letter to Silverio and the two decide to use it to blackmail Don
Roque. They threaten to show the letter to Doña Luisa unless
the abbé gets permission from Doña Luisa for the cousins to
marry. As an added inducement, Don Roque is promised a sum
of money for moving expenses. He does as he is told, telling
Doña Luisa that he wants to join a monastery.

The coyness of Cecelia sets the tone for the play. There is
no effort to make Don Roque into a melodramatic villain. Cecelia
treats Silverio very coquettishly. Despite her youth, she is far
shrewder than her cousin. The interest in the letter almost completely dominates the second act. First, Silverio sees her kissing
the letter and asks about its contents. Next, she spends some time
convincing him that if he really loves her he will not show this
curiosity which seems so close to distrust. Just as soon as she gets

him to promise not to try to read the letter, she insists on having him read it. Then she must explain its importance to him since he is too dense to see her plan. Finally, when the blackmail scene is taking place, whenever Don Roque seems to hesitate in promising to propose to Luisa the marriage of the cousins, the letter is presented so that he and the audience can see it. This action serves to prompt him to the proper decision for the two lovers.

The other play, *El licenciado Farfulla* (*Lawyer Farfulla*), tends even more toward farce. Instead of being a real lawyer, Farfulla is a crook with great cunning and resourcefulness. He comes to an inn and meets Perico, an employee at the inn whom he has known from earlier escapades. He offers to go into partnership with Perico, promising to share their gains and planning to double-cross Perico in the process. Any guest of the inn is a potential victim. The best one is Lesmes, a very naive merchant who is in love with Doña Isabel, a foreign lady. Farfulla promises to serve Lesmes as go-between and "borrows" his coat to be able to present a better appearance. He also persuades Lesmes that he has occult powers, and pretends first to change him into a staircase and then to make him invisible. Meanwhile, he tells others that he is a silversmith and gathers their metal products, announcing that he is going to clean them. Farfulla arranges with Perico to hide his stolen goods in a small closet and Farfulla takes the key. He is almost ready to escape with the spoils, but he has underestimated Perico, who was suspicious of him from the beginning and who has a second key. Perico sounds the alarm and tells Farfulla that all is lost and that he has thrown everything into the well so that they can't get caught. While everyone has gone off yelling for the law, the magistrate comes in and sees Farfulla, who tells him that he is a tailor and that the thief is a short, fat man. (Lesmes answers that description.) Farfulla escapes temporarily in the magistrate's cloak. Perico shows everyone the stolen goods and a constable soon returns with the news that Farfulla has been caught.

Cruz's farce, composed in zarzuela form, has only one act and is not divided into scenes, although it is a relatively long work. Don Ramón might have been encouraged to compose the light farce more often. He comes closer to fulfilling the needs of this form than of any other except that of the sainete.

## V *Summary*

The conventional criticism of Ramón de la Cruz normally dismisses his longer plays as having no literary value. The review of these plays which has just been completed might serve to diminish somewhat the harshness of this judgment, but not to make major changes in it. In his original works, the idealism was too superficial and the dramatic situations too commonplace to hold lasting interest. Apparently he made good use of the zarzuela form and of all music and dance accessories. He proved to be a competent translator of French and Italian plays, but the plays that he chose to translate were often no better than his own; even when he chose to translate plays by highly skilled foreign dramatists, he selected some of their lesser plays. The continued, even though minor, popularity of these dramas during his lifetime was probably due to the reputation that he built with his sainetes and to the fact that Don Ramón's full-length plays, mediocre as they were, were fully the equal of those of any of his rivals.

# CHAPTER 10

## *Evaluators of Ramón de la Cruz*

THIS chapter offers some of the criticism of Don Ramón through a selection of the opinions of the scholars who have shown most interest in evaluating his work. They bridge the time from his day to ours, and, coming from widely differing backgrounds and orientations, they naturally vary in their opinions of the value and the values of his work. In the case of the sainetes, these opinions are more polarized than usual in literary evaluations, partly because of the literary quarrels of Don Ramón's day, but more fundamentally because of differing attitudes toward the intrinsic value of the one-act play as a genre.

### I  *Opinions of Don Ramón's Contemporaries*

Tomás de Iriarte was not the most disinterested critic we might have chosen to begin this evaluation. As a very young man, he joined the anti-Cruz group, echoing and amplifying the voice of his older brother, Bernardo. As we examine his thought, we must consider the criticism in the heat as well as the light in which it was written. Iriarte's views are important to us, however, for two special reasons: First, he was a good representative of the point of view of the well-educated, talented person who fostered the French tradition in Spain, and second, his chief barb occurred in the heart of his own most significant work, his *Fábulas* (*Fables*). Since the fables were written as entertainment for all intellectually minded people rather than for specialists in a particular area of Spanish literature, the ideas that he expressed reached a wider public and their venom lasted longer. He introduced his fable number twenty-eight in this manner; we quote from Cotarelo:[1]

"The foolish common man always looks upon the good and the bad with equal esteem. I give him the worst, which is what he praises."

144

In this way a writer of indecent farces was excusing his errors and a sly poet who heard him responded in the following terms: "His master gave the humble ass some straw and he said to him, 'Take it since you are happy with it.' He told him this so many times that one day the ass got angry and replied, 'I take what you give me, but, unjust man, do you think that I like nothing but straw? Give me grain and you will see how well I eat.'"

Iriarte's criticism unfortunately insults the public as much as it does Don Ramón. It does proclaim that even the asinine public can be educated to appreciate a higher form of literature than it usually gets, but it reveals at the same time its author's own uneasiness. Iriarte has not demonstrated that Cruz's fare is of low quality; he has merely expressed the accusation in such a clever way that his reader will laugh and forget the fact that no truth has been demonstrated.

Despite Iriarte's wrath, there is no reason to doubt the sincerity of his criticism. A poet almost always has the feeling that the popular writer is shallow, that he himself is writing for posterity or for the ages, and that his more popular rival's fame will prove ephemeral. One may recall that Cervantes himself had similar feelings about the comedy of Lope de Vega, and although he managed to express his feelings with a great deal more diplomacy, his words are usually remembered as those of prophecy gone astray. It is a commonplace to observe that contemporaries cannot judge how posterity will look upon a writer, but for Spain a certain generalization will be peculiarly valid: the Spaniard does not disdain the popular. Since he praises the "flesh and bone" as the essence of manhood, he naturally dislikes intellectual snobbishness. Spanish literature and art always seem to have a popular inspiration, and it is not perfected through a process of distillation for intellectual purity as it is in some other countries. The popular image permeates the finished product.

Iriarte's fellow writer of fables, Samaniego, agrees with Iriarte that Don Ramón's theater is bad. He inquires: Is it possible that he is never going to picture a physician who is not ignorant and of vile motivation, a lawyer who is not a liar, a scribe who is not a falsifier or a bailiff who is not a thief?"[2] Samaniego could have found just the examples that he asks about, but they would in most cases be inconspicuous. A comic character must have some quality about him that the public can laugh at. Moreover,

Samaniego's criticism is too selective. Don Ramón attacks the character weaknesses and idiosyncracies of all kinds of people.

It would not serve our present purpose to offer extensive examples of literary attacks upon Don Ramón by his contemporaries, but mention has already been made (See Chapter 2) of the Italian critic, Signorelli, whose criticism of Cruz was especially unjust. The Italian apparently got his information and prejudices from the *tertulia* called *Fonda de San Sebastián* founded by the elder Moratín. For Signorelli the sainetes of Cruz have characters so grotesque that they cause tedium, and he claims that Don Ramón's style was naturally lowly and fell to the ground whenever he tried to make it rise. The Italian reported a lack of popular appeal in Don Ramón's zarzuelas but did not present any evidence of this.

Don Ramón usually tried to ignore his critics or to satirize them in a general way in his sainetes, but in the prologue to his edition of his works, he defended himself specifically against Signorelli's attacks, and Signorelli replied in the second edition of his own works. The Italian probably deserved only to be ignored and Don Ramón may be accused of a trace of prejudice against foreigners. According to Cotarelo,[3] Signorelli was so ignorant that he did not realize that Don Ramón's *Manolo* was a parody.

One of the most important early evaluators of Ramón de la Cruz was Leandro Fernández de Moratín. His father, Nicolás, had been one of Don Ramón's most bitter antagonists. The younger Moratín represented a conservative Classical bent, but from his time perspective and his own broad view of the Spanish theater he was able to offer a rather sympathetic opinion of Don Ramón:

Ramón de la Cruz was the only one of whom it could be said that at that time he understood the essence of good comedy: because, dedicating himself particularly to the composition of one-act pieces called sainetes, he was able to substitute for the sloven and vulgar courses of our ancient *entremeses* the exact and humorous imitation of the modern customs of the people. Often he lost sight of the moral purpose that he should have given to his little stories; he lent to vice (and even crime) such flattering color that those actions of which modesty and virtue disapprove and which the laws punish with severity are made to appear as mere guile and mischief. He never learned how to compose a dramatic combination of true grandeur, of a fully sustained interest, a plot without a natural denouement; his figures never form a group arranged artistically, but, examined separately, almost all are imitated from nature with admirable fidelity. This gift, which is not common, together with a spirited dialogue, humorous and facile (rather than correct), gave his little comic pieces the applause that they truly merited.[4]

We do not see in the younger Moratín's views any large carry-over of the quarrels of his father's time. The negative aspects of his criticism represent rather his own views of organization and decorum. However, Moratín recognized that Don Ramón had the natural gift for comedy which his contemporaries lacked and in this recognition was found the heart of the matter. Anything else that is said, pro or con, becomes almost ancillary to this main point. In fact, Moratín's ability to see the comic genius of Ramón de la Cruz, in spite of his different background and tastes, is a mark of the great ability of both Cruz as a writer and Moratín as a critic.

## II  *The Judgment of Later Critics*

A generation after Moratín, Agustín Durán edited 120 sainetes in a work that we cited in Chapter 1. This was the first really important edition of Cruz's works since the author's own, and an edition which stands today among the three main sources of Don Ramón's productions. In Durán's introduction he includes the comments of several critics. One of special interest is that of Juan Eugenio Hartzenbusch, who uses *El careo de los majos* (*The Confrontation of the Majos*) to illustrate the variety of Don Ramón's wit. He starts with a brief sample:

—Gentlemen, let the jackass pass.
—Go ahead, son.
   He follows with a subtler one:
   CONSTABLE. Who are these gentlemen?
   OLAYA. I don't know a thing. But if these men are known it is all right.
   DIONISIO. Except for me. I don't know any of my relations, not even my father.
   CONSTABLE. Not even your father? That's strange.
   DIONISIO. "That's strange?" Would you swear who yours was?

CONSTABLE. Of course I would swear it.
DIONISIO. It's a question of conscience. Mine is more delicate.[5]

Pérez Galdós in 1871 wrote a long essay, "Don Ramón de la Cruz y su época,"[6] the first half of which is a blanket condemnation of the eighteenth century in Spain. Galdós had evidently studied the century with some care, and of course, considerable bias. He consigned most eighteenth-century authors to what amounts to a ninth circle in an inferno of pure boredom. The authors with a modicum of talent were placed in a limbo by Galdós' special grace since for him the century itself, with its dulling atmosphere, was the excuse for all their defects. He then stated that Ramón de la Cruz was the only one of national spirit. The liberal Galdós sees the genius of Don Ramón as he gives us a plausible and vividly dramatized picture of the emptiness of the age as he saw it and contrasts it with the view of the *maja* as the only genuine survival of the earlier Spanish civilization. For Galdós, Don Ramón would have emerged as a true genius but for the damnable age in which he lived.

If Galdós is exaggerating the virtues of Don Ramón, he may find some motivation for it since he saw in his time a neglect of Cruz's sainetes. Apparently the type of appeal of Ramón de la Cruz is such that it must be refostered from time to time to save it from desuetude. I would like to have been able to ask Galdós —in the interesting even though futile game of literary hypothesis —if he could conceive that Ramón de la Cruz could have needed his age and environment as much to bring out his special genius as the age needed him to dramatize it.

The most important scholarship on Ramón de la Cruz has been that of Don Emilio Cotarelo y Mori, of frequent reference in this book. His main accomplishment has not been in evaluating Don Ramón, but rather in facilitating the enjoyment and evaluation by others. He composed the only really complete and authoritative biography and, through the two volumes of the *Nueva biblioteca de autores españoles* (*New Collection of Spanish Authors*), has edited 163 sainetes. His plans called for twice that number, but he was not able to complete them, and no one has undertaken this task. While Cotarelo's manner is always scholarly and objective, he can be placed with those who consider Don Ramón to be a skilled dramatist and a realistic observer of

Spanish life under Charles III. That Don Emilio did not have the same prejudice as Galdós toward the eighteenth century can be seen in his dispassionate view of it in *Don Tomás de Iriarte y su época* (*Tomás de Iriarte and His Age*), a monumental work treating of Don Ramón's time through a rival's life and works.

While Don Emilio was editing the sainetes in Spain, two American authors were doing their part to maintain interest in Ramón de la Cruz: Messrs. Charles E. Kany and Arthur Hamilton. Like Cotarelo, Kany was interested in seeing that Cruz's manuscripts were edited. He turned out a score of these, five of them prepared for reading in second-year language classes in the United States. Mr. Kany enables us to get his views of Don Ramón in a somewhat indirect manner. One of the sainetes which he edited is: *Lo que es del agua, el agua se lo lleva* (*If Something Is Made of Water, Water Takes It Away*). While editing this sainete, he expresses his belief that it was not by Don Ramón. His argument is: "First, since the subject matter is a popular tale it is not characteristic of the manner of Cruz, who used to copy what he saw without having any ready made plot, but rather allowing what little plot there is to burst forth spontaneously from the animation of the crowds. This sainete seems to have a rather well developed exposition, which gives us to know all of the principal characters by means of questions from Pilatos and the replies of his son. Cruz is not guided in his sainetes by the construction rules of comedy, and his characters, without being announced, enter, talk, and make themselves known by their own actions and speeches."[7] Kany further adds that such farcical elements of the sainete as the son's throwing water on his wife and beating her are coarse things more representative of the older state of the sainete than of Don Ramón's plays. He concludes that the value of Don Ramón's work is precisely in refining comedy to remove these gross elements. He admits that Don Ramón's earlier work held some of these features, but insists that his later plays lacked these elements.

My purpose in reproducing this analysis is not to agree or disagree with Mr. Kany in the specific question of the authorship of this sainete—many of whose elements are comparable to Don Ramón's *The Coachman of M. Corneta*—but rather to take advantage of his keen analysis of the unique manner of Don Ramón's stage craft. It is a little startling to think that lack of planning and organization is a positive virtue in a dramatic work, but Mr. Kany makes it sound convincing.

Mr. Hamilton's major scholastic work on Ramón de la Cruz is *A Study of Spanish Manners, 1750–1800*, taken from the sainetes. The "manners" include daily life, dress, home decorations, the characters, and their mannerisms; in short, a very thorough treatment of Spanish life at that time. While the formality of this study contrasts with the extreme informality of the plays, Hamilton's report is far from dull. Elsewhere, he has written of Don Ramón's indebtedness to Molière[8] and of his efforts as a reformer.[9] Mr. Hamilton admits that Ramón de la Cruz did not succeed as a social reformer—in the more formal sense—and that there seemed to be an inverse correlation between the efforts at reform and the popularity of his plays. His purpose, however, is to refute the idea that Ramón de la Cruz had no serious purpose in writing the sainetes. He feels that the selection that Cruz made for editing a part of his literary production was an effort to stress his social purpose and that Don Ramón learned with great difficulty that the less he placed formal stress upon reform, the more effective was his play, the more poignant the message it contained.

The point of view that Ramón de la Cruz is unjustly neglected, a diamond in the rough, or that his is the most authentic voice and himself the playwright of most genuine talent in the eighteenth century is not always maintained by twentieth-century critics. For example, in their history of the Spanish theater, Díaz de Escóvar and Lasso de la Vega,[10] in a thorough study of all phases of the Spanish stage, claim that the work of Ramón de la Cruz is of poor quality. They describe him as an opportunist with more malice than prudence, with more severity than urbanity. When he tried to rise above the sainete to picture the higher forms of drama, he produced pale and insipid comedies. Then, as if feeling that their statements are too harsh, the critics give Don Ramón credit for very effective satire. They finish by saying that, in spite of his *incorrecciones*, he is to be praised as the first restorer of national drama and for giving his satire in such a way that villainy is not extolled. (This last statement is in peculiar contrast to Moratín's on the moral impact.) Their view seems to be a lament, not that he was not better known, but that his talent was not devoted to a higher genre. They also bring in an element that has not been stressed up to this point. While giving praise to the sainetes, they imply that the sainete in essence is of a lower order than full-length high comedy and point out, quite correctly, that our dramatist was not able to make the transition or ascent to the full-length play.

One especially perceptive critic of Spanish drama in Angel Valbuena Prat.[11] Sr. Valbuena suggests that we should separate two considerations which in his opinion have been fused: the quite considerable value of Don Ramón's work in the process of making an age understandable to other ages, and the ageless aesthetic evaluation of his comic art. Valbuena does not believe that the latter has been sufficiently studied; therefore his own views must be somewhat tentative. He feels that, if the works of Don Ramón were subjected to an extensive and careful analysis, the conclusion would be that he is quite inferior to the picture of him now presented by Ramonophiles. He finds him somewhat disappointing in versification, style, and grace.

As representative of the current viewpoint with regard to Ramón de la Cruz, I have selected a work by Richard E. Chandler and Kessel Schwartz, *A New History of Spanish Literature*.[12] They give him a compliment, perhaps unintentionally, by devoting to him the same amount of space given to Calderón. There is nothing novel in their evaluation, but they do an excellent job of reporting most of the observations that have already been made: the importance of Cruz's work in its historical and documentary accuracy, the popularity of his plays at the time they were staged, the democratic nature of Spanish drama, the contrast between the drama of Don Ramón and that of his contemporaries, and special consideration of the *tranches de vie* which are the vehicle of his humor and criticism. Only his versification receives their adverse criticism.

From this brief look at the judgments of these commentators, we have adduced two generalizations which may be useful. The first of these is that when we have removed the judgments based upon strong emotional reaction or upon ignorance, we find that Don Ramón has an undisputed place of importance in his century. He makes his epoch come to life with characters who tell their own story in their own way. For better or for worse, he preserved the national Spanish spirit at a time when most literary leaders were working hard to destroy or transform it. He was the most talented comedy writer of his century.

Our second generalization is that there exists a divergence wider than usual concerning the overall aesthetic worth of his work. For some, the unorthodox manner of his dramatic technique is praiseworthy evidence of the Spanish spirit's breaking the shackles of convention. For others it represents only the triumph of a man who was operating in a culturally inferior milieu, a man who occasionally strove to move up to greater things, but who realized eventually that he lacked the genius to carry it out.

# CHAPTER 11

# *Recapitulation and Conclusion*

D O we now have a basis for a full personal evaluation of the
literary accomplishments of Don Ramón de la Cruz Cano
y Olmedilla, or do we need to wait for further light from the
critics and scholars? One can certainly lament that Cotarelo was
unable to finish his proposed task of a virtually complete edition
of the sainetes. Until all the evidence is gathered where the
scholarly world can see it, there is always the chance, even
though a small one, that some important observation is waiting
in an unpublished manuscript for an astute researcher to bring
it out for us. Students of stylistics and versification, armed with
the computer, may yet bring data for our consideration which
will be helpful in deciding Don Ramón's net worth. Conceivably,
biographical facts not yet brought to light may be the reward of
some academic sleuth's diligence and luck. Yet even if such dis-
coveries are made, it is unlikely to change criticism in any fundamental way. For all practical considerations, we have all the
sources of information that we need and have had enough time
to handle them and reflect upon them. Our decisions may be
wrong or biased, but there is no reason why they should be tentative or hedged. This evaluation will not be final because such
decisions never are. Opinions and tastes will forever vary from
person to person and fluctuate from age to age, but I believe that
I should at least attempt a total estimate of Don Ramón's dramatic achievement.

## I  *Biography*

The biography of Don Ramón, unfortunately, is not a good
place to look to determine the worth of his production. He was
a small man; small in physical stature, in his job as a government
clerk, and in his socio-economic standing. He loomed a little

larger only in his influence over the theater of his time and in his ability to handle himself in a literary quarrel. There was steadfastness in his devotion to the cause of Spanish traditionalism in the face of the strong current of French influence, but he showed no heroic qualities in a major key. During the period of the influence of the Count of Aranda, he tried to adapt his dramatic art to the political climate, but not so much so as to fawn upon potential benefactors or to abandon his principles for the sake of patronage or for fear of the suppression of his work. There was little dynamism in his personality; he was inferior in this respect to the elder Moratín. One can name his enemies, but his friends, who must have been numerous, were largely anonymous except for a few casual patrons. He left no followers to carry on his work. His biography is colorless.

Ramón de la Cruz displayed no remarkable erudition. He presumably attended the University of Salamanca briefly. He knew French and Italian well enough to translate plays from those languages, and had learned several of the dialects of his country well enough to mimic them. He showed a knowledge of scattered bits of ancient literature, but he gave no evidence of breadth of view or of philosophic depth. He depended much more upon his powers of observation than those of erudition or introspection. The keenness of his observations on life was not sharpened by travel; he was born, lived, and died in Madrid, and the only other place in which he lived for a considerable period of time was Ceuta, a city which influenced his works only in his calling attention in his sainetes to its penal institutions.

Ramón de la Cruz did not even have any interesting vices or idiosyncrasies. His life seemed to have been free of public scandal or private intrigue. He had brothers, a wife who survived him, and children, but nowhere does his personal life enter his theatrical world, unless, of course, it has done so in ways which have gone undetected. Only in the general sense that he wrote out of what he himself was can he be said to have put himself into his plays.

To find the real Ramón de la Cruz is not easy since neither his biography nor his plays tell us much about the inner man. Obvious to me is a comparison with Cervantes, although I recognize that there is a danger in carrying the comparison too far. Both men wrote in a day when the conventional literary milieu was one of shallow idealism. Both tried to write in a way that would please the public, and posterity agrees that neither man gave us lasting value until he broke away from the form that was in vogue to write about his real feelings. Cervantes certainly, and Cruz probably, felt emotionally attracted to writing within an idealistic setting. They chose to believe that the world is better than it is or at least that the better side of human nature can be encouraged to assert itself. Both men eventually devoted their efforts to writing realistically but sympathetically of the common man, and found that true idealism rests on a realistic base. Cruz was actually closer to the common man and seemed less patronizing in dealing with him. Cervantes reserved his deepest thoughts for Don Quixote, but Don Ramón, on the few occasions when his emotions approached anything like the depth of tragedy, searched the soul of the common man or woman.

In spite of his serving as the voice of freedom for the eighteenth century in Spain, Don Ramón was essentially a conservative man. In *The Happy Test* he showed that a wise uncle might be a better judge of character than a young niece, even for choosing her own husband. In several plays Cruz objected to a person's party-going after a very brief period of mourning. He showed sympathy for the lower classes, but set them down heavily if they forgot their places and tried to act like snobs. He wrote sainetes in which a wealthy man tried to correct various flaws in individuals by forceful means. The attempt always failed, but the failure was attributed to the stubbornness of human nature rather than to his using the wrong approach. Don Ramón fought the worship of foreign influences almost to the point of xenophobia. The fact that what he was combatting was new to Spain made him necessarily a defender of the old. He was maneuvered into a position of opposing most of what was sophisticated and urbane in his country.

He seemed not only conservative, but also somewhat introverted. His ability to observe human nature and to dramatize it without injecting his own personality suggests that he was not a good mixer. He could concentrate upon his task of observing a crowd without having to participate in its activities. If he had felt more at ease in a crowd, he would have had less motivation for examining it critically.

Apparently we must be content with examining his thoughts by this inferential method, unsatisfactory though it is. We have no diary and no letters into which we may pry, and the introduction to his published works gives us only general impressions of what he presumably felt. I say this somewhat *pro forma* since his literary legacy does not need his biography for its message to be quite clear.

Two groups of helpers should be cited for their contributions to Don Ramón's success. For his zarzuelas and musical comedies he had the collaboration of talented musical composers. To all appearances he worked well with them. We have given but brief attention to this aspect of his work since, as has been demonstrated, only his sainetes are of wide interest today.

Of greater significance is his rapport with actors and actresses. The elder Moratín saw the direct raw power of the cast when it refused to perform two of his plays. Who can guess what subtle and unconscious powers the actors had with a play's success or failure? Don Ramón had the actors and actresses very much in mind when he wrote a sainete, so much so that he normally used the name of the player he intended to play the part rather than the part itself when he designated a name for the character. He wrote a number of plays which took the spectator backstage and even had several in which an actor's name appeared in the title. Occasionally the script would have an action whose meaning was lost upon those who did not know the actors, their marital partners, something of their private lives, and their special characteristics. The atmosphere thus created even carries over to the printed page and the twentieth century, for one gets the feeling that Don Ramón was completely relaxed as he wrote. With some playwrights, writing for a particular actor is a limitation; for Don Ramón, it was a liberation. The fact that he was able to project a zest for life, a feeling that he was enjoying the plays while writing them, should be listed among his assets.

## II   *General Characteristics of His Comic Art*

Despite our negative conclusions from his biography, it is obvious from his literary production that Ramón de la Cruz had important talents: mastery of stage techniques and timing, keen powers of observation, and a sure sense of the comedy of life. His plays had a vivid persuasiveness that his personality lacked, and he was fortunate in having well organized and talented theater companies to implement it. He had an inner strength which impelled him to show, in his unique way, the surface decay of Spanish society and the teeming humanity trying to live in the social smog. Thus the evidence of his worth is found almost exclusively in the examination of the sainetes themselves.

One of the most important qualities that Don Ramón shows in his sainetes is his fairness. Of course he has been accused of bias. His enemies claim strong and grossly unjust prejudice. Impartial commentators seem to perceive a mild bias in favor of the lower classes and against the *petimetre* society. It may be true that his sympathies lay with the lower classes, but Don Ramón was after laughs, and both the *majo* and the *payo* could say ruefully he did not "pull his punches" when he pictured them. There was considerable sting in the portraits of the abbés, *cortejos,* and *petimetres,* but there was little bitterness. Occasionally, very discreet members of that society were represented on his stage, perhaps to show contrast to the indiscretions of the others. Don Ramón wants to ridicule bad or silly practices rather than attack a class of people, but it must be acknowledged that these superficial traits serve to create the *petimetre.* A person is a *petimetre* through choice, not through birth.

There is more pathos in the treatment of the lower classes. This is as it should be. We recall that Don Quixote asked Sancho to show the poor more compassion but not more justice than the rich. To me, pathos reaches its zenith in the fatalism of *The Fritter.* It is a special kind of pathos reserved for the little people whose tragedies do not have the grandeur of the Classic stage, but are based upon the same kind of emotion and character and seem to the characters themselves to have the same moral mandate from forces outside the will. The tragedy is almost as great in the absurdity of the costly wedding in the trilogy of the barber. On the other hand, there is also pathos in the plight of the *petimetre* who goes on partying in the *sarao* trilogy with Spartan resignation and little sense of enjoyment. In this respect the *petimetre* is comparable to the squire in *Lazarillo de Tormes.* Both are slaves of the social mores, which demand of them more than they can possibly produce.

Don Ramón gives the society of his day a comic treatment. If that society were capable of being treated in any other way, there should have been writers to do the task. Since the efforts at Classic tragedy produced few plays as worthy of preservation as Don Ramón's burlesque tragedy, *Manolo,* it is reasonable to assume that the society could not inspire the lofty sentiments that produced Sophocles, Shakespeare, or Racine. If the society still held the strong religious, nationalistic, and personal convictions of the Spanish Golden Age, it might have been expressed by such plays as *La Estrella de Sevilla* (*The Star of Seville*), *La prudencia en la mujer* (*Prudence in a Woman*) or *El alcalde de Zalamea* (*The Mayor of Zalamea*), but nothing remotely resembling these plays appeared, with the single exception of García de la Huerta's *Raquel.* The whole society was behaving abnormally and only the burlesque treatment made it vivid, real, and vibrant in literature. Don Ramón's antagonists, who considered themselves sophisticated and urbane, would have received with dismay and disbelief the idea that posterity might consider them the nearsighted ones and Don Ramón the one who could see their Age in its perspective for Spanish history.

The comic treatment naturally distorts the picture. If we take the *petimetre* society from the stage to society as it really was, the number of serious people concerned with important moral problems is greatly surpassed by those who are caught in the whirlwind of superficial social matters of dress and entertainment. Don Ramón was not prepared to fill the emptiness of a vacuous society by a positive philosophy or a plan for a richly meaningful way of life. He could only show how empty the symbols of that society were. Since he was writing plays to entertain, since he was aiming to destroy the images of these people, and to show how lifeless those images were, he should not be accused of having written history, true or false. Historians, of course, find this work pure gold in their studies of this society through Don Ramón, but they have the duty to interpret it as evidence drawn from fiction.

Ramón de la Cruz claims that Truth dictates as he writes. Truth for man is a many-faceted thing. For the philosopher it may be an exercise in logic. For the reporter it is the accurate observation and transcription of events he has observed. Don Ramón's statement seems like that of a mystic who has just had communion with a goddess; actually, however, he was seeking an intuitive artistic truth. He was writing fiction, and our estimate of his worth should be made primarily and fundamentally upon his skill in fiction. His contribution to the study of the culture of his times, therefore, is secondary and derivative. As a dramatist he has written about two worlds, the world of his longer plays and that of his sainetes. In the former he is writing in a milieu created by other writers and he offers little that is original. In the sainete, however, he has created his own world. He has touched his Adam and breathed life into him. Paradoxically, when Don Ramón was writing Truth as he saw it, he was far more creative and imaginative than when he was writing works of fantasy. Therefore we find merit in his sainetes today, not because true pictures are essentially superior to fanciful ones, but because Ramón de la Cruz could handle a realistic milieu far more skillfully than a fantastic one.

In Don Ramón's stage there is little effort to provide motivation for entrances and exits, and little need for it since the characters seem to act autonomously. In this respect Don Ramón seems to have anticipated the Impressionist school. Theoretically, the technique is easy. With the movie camera it would seem even easier for us today. In practice it is much harder. As the characters appear and disappear so haphazardly, Don Ramón must be inside each one, seeing at least the broad outlines of every character's soul. The character must be able to communicate instantly with the spectator without introduction or explanation. The author must even consider the spectator himself, for he must be able to understand almost instinctively the picture that is being unfolded. The ability to understand human nature intuitively is a great gift, but the ability to give dramatic expression to it is a rarer one.

Impressionism in itself is not enough. There must be oversimplification without sacrificing the impressionistic feelings. The human mind is naturally selective and the dramatist must be an astute preselector hopefully without the spectator's being aware of it. If the playwright succeeds, his characters take on two paradoxical qualities, stylization and natural individuality. On the one hand the character seems almost allegorical in the portrayal of a type, say the abbé or the *cortejo*. On the other hand, the character seems to be drawn from life itself almost as a personal acquaintance of the spectator. Don Ramón had a

talent comparable to that of Cervantes in this respect and, not
very surprisingly, shared with Cervantes the ability to write an
*entremés* or sainete and the tendency to flounder in efforts at
full-length drama.

One other important quality characterizes Don Ramón: a
comedian's love for the man he is laughing at. There is an element of cruelty in any form of making fun of our fellow man, but
the writer who accomplishes true comedy knows instinctively
and lovingly where to stop. Having had his fun, he is ready to
forget, forgive, and expect to be forgiven. He dances in and out
among the holy relics and sacred cows of life, tearing apart the
sham with which we distort many of our holy symbols, but leaving the essence there, sturdy and strong. If Don Ramón had
hated the *petimetre,* he could not have made fun of him to such
widespread applause, for underneath the *petimetre* is a man.
After Don Ramón's humor has been wrought upon him, he is
more of a man.

Comedy itself is measure. It takes cognizance of the fallibility
and inconsistency of all men. It makes fun of those who for
whatever reason are acting oddly. It therefore deals with matters
relatively and calls for reasonable rather than idealistic life.
Tragedy may imply a perfect standard against which to measure
human conduct. Therefore comedy is the enemy of conduct
which is exaggerated rather than fundamentally wrong. The
writer of comedy operates by dramatizing this conduct in an even
more exaggerated manner and by removing the qualifying and
mitigating circumstances, but the lesson of his humor is to seek
reasonable moderation in everything.

Ramón de la Cruz was very human, so some of his sainetes
display much more bitterness than others. A few express tragedies
of life which seem to have no solution because of the stubbornness of human nature. Others show simply that the author is
momentarily too blinded by emotional reaction to the assaults of
his enemies, but even the satires directed against particular
enemies have some restraint about them. The plays which show
his counterattacks upon his enemies have usually attracted more
attention than their intrinsic value warrants. Caustic wit is not
Don Ramón at his best.

### III   *The Sainete Reflects His Age*

As most successful writers, Don Ramón understood the weaknesses of his own times and knew how to satirize them effectively. Consider a contrast in times as reflected by Cruz and by Francisco de Quevedo. Quevedo attacked what was false in his times through his *Sueños* (*Visions*). His erstwhile victim, the Golden Age *galán,* was ridiculed at his most vulnerable point, his misplaced pride. We see the hollow quality of the *galán* as Quevedo tries hard to cut through his defenses to make him see himself. The *galán* did maintain some residual strength since he was a genuine Spaniard. The *petimetre* on the other hand, was not a genuine Spaniard, but a French imitator. Don Ramón did not need the caustic wit of Quevedo; he had but to give a gentle tug at the carpet under the *petimetre's* feet to send him sprawling. Each man was the more effective for having been in the age in which he lived.

Probably we remember Ramón de la Cruz best for his satire of the bourgeois society, but he was not concerned entirely with the upper classes. In fact, it is more natural to find humor among the lower classes. A large part of his success on the stage is his understanding of the *majos.* To the extent that he found farce his most efficient vehicle for the expression of comedy, he saw that the ordinary man is a good subject for humor, since the ordinary person's lack of sophistication is easy to capture, and the various ways that he tries to conceal truth from others or from himself are easy to disclose. But Don Ramón's humor makes us remember the *majo,* who was as distinctive for eighteenth-century Spain as was the *petimetre.* As the preserver of Spanish tradition, he had a power vis-à-vis the upper classes that commoners seldom have. His tastes were blatantly and militantly Spanish in contrast to the foreignness of the *petimetre's.* The trouble was that it was unnatural for him to be a style setter. He was placed in the artificial position of having to oppose, for the sake of opposition itself, the equally artificial position of the *petimetre.* His dress and conduct became exaggerated to oppose other exaggerations.

An example of this negative kind of influence is the contrast between the *cortejo* and the *majo.* The *cortejo* served his lady under rules of conduct which were rather rigid for both. He exercised considerable control over a *petimetra* while posing as

162

her slave. At the same time, the *majo* became quite dependent
upon the *maja* while posing as her master. The *majo*, although
opposing the *cortejo* in the name of Spanish traditionalism, un-
consciously imitated him in that both made a virtue of idleness.
On the stage we often see a *maja* working. If a young man is
working, he is not designated a *majo*, and incidentally, he is not
working very hard.

Don Ramón's satire of the *majo* has caused a curious thing; it
has raised the *majo's* status by giving him a name and an image.
In the farce of earlier times, he would have been one of the non-
descript poor. With Don Ramón, he has acquired status. On the
other hand, Don Ramón never spared him. He often showed the
cowardice underneath his bluster and the emptiness of purpose
that accompanied his physical idleness. He showed the *majo*
returning from prison, fighting over a trifle, and acting pettily in
a thousand ways. The same kind of treatment which felled the
*petimetre* propped up the *majo*.

If this is true of the *majo*, it is even more true of the *maja*.
There was some validity in Galdós' statement that she was the
real preserver of the ancient Spanish personality and spirit. She
is not idealized by Don Ramón. Her fights and quarrels mark her
as anything but a lady in the usual sense. Both the *petimetre*
and the *majo* force her to fight almost physically to live and keep
her self-respect. She alone in the world of Don Ramón works
hard. With all her faults, she is almost never accused of being
weak or hypocritical.

The setting for the sainetes is Madrid, the Madrid that Don
Ramón knew and that the theatergoer knew. It was the streets,
the houses, the marketplace, the outskirts of the city. The time
could be a workday or holiday; early morning, or late at night.
The action could involve scenes as commonplace as the chestnut
vendor's stand or as unusual as the entrance of an elephant. The
realism of the atmosphere strengthened the realism of the characterizations.

The significance of the plots varies. Some, such as *The Fritter*,
are well thought out. Others, such as *Main Square*, have virtually
no plot, even though they may have careful planning. A few,
such as *La Petra y la Juana*, seem to have no plot until the end,
and there a clever speech ties things together for us and shows
us a moving theme. Don Ramón's apparent lack of emphasis

upon plot development is no limitation for one who examines his total production and is so moved that he finds there an affinity to the folk epic in spite of the antiheroic qualities of many individuals in the sainetes. There is no epic hero and no heroic saga. The epic usually causes the reader to love the people by loving the hero who speaks and acts for them. Here the people speak and act for themselves. The hero cannot be found, but there is an inescapable feeling that there is heroism hidden in Don Ramón's world because of its openly expressed love of life.

Heroism normally means combat. The war in this case was a "cold" war between the traditional Spaniards and those who felt that the French were the arbiters of good taste. The traditionalists, poor, disorganized, uneducated, with instincts rather than reason or rhetoric to guide them, were virtually helpless. The *petimetres*, organized in salons, educated in foreign culture, and placed in positions of authority, were the rulers, and in a minor way the oppressors. Only in the theater did the traditionalists have a major rallying point and only in the meek Ramón de la Cruz did they have a champion. Eventually the traditionalists won, but it was the outrages of Napoleon, not the quips of Ramón de la Cruz which killed the *petimetre*. We can thank Don Ramón for preserving the memory of his heyday.

## IV  *The Longer Plays*

As we have seen, throughout his life Don Ramón wrote plays other than sainetes: short comedies, zarzuelas, full-length comedies and translations, including plays he called tragedies, most of which may hardly be called that. Fairly early in life he realized that he was far more skilled and more successful in the sainete than in the other forms. While in his later years he concentrated upon the sainete, he continued also to write longer plays, and when, near the end of his life, he published ten volumes of his works, he had more pages for his full-length plays than he did for the sainetes.

There is a special irony in all of this. We have just pictured Don Ramón de la Cruz, a quixotic champion of the people in their cultural struggle to preserve their own customs against the oppressive French cultural invasion. We have suggested that with the greatest of ease Cruz made comic targets of his opposition, showing all the world that the true Spaniard found his soul's sustenance in his own soil and his own tradition. And yet, he did not completely convince himself that he was right. He must have had recurring feelings that a three-act play was, by definition, better than a sainete. At least it provided him greater financial reward. A part, but only a relatively small part, of this non-sainete production was stimulated by his desire to conform to the standards of the Count of Aranda. He was never quite able to convince himself that his sainetes, in the judgment of history, would be found superior to his other productions, and he was anxious to prove to his enemies that he could write in their style as well as they could.

He succeeded. Don Ramón's comedies, however mediocre, were the equal of those of any Spanish writer of this time, but they should have been and could have been so much better. Don Ramón had two distinct manners: the realism of his sainetes and the fantasy and superficial idealism of his comedies. He engaged in this double-think all of his life. When writing sainetes, he was writing about life as he was able to observe it. When writing comedies, he was writing escape literature as he was able to dream it and as he could observe in the writings of his contemporaries. One wonders what might have resulted if he had really applied his talent for realistic drama to the composition of full-length plays!

Alas, one is constrained to write of what he did rather than what he might have accomplished. In *The Story of Briseis* he dramatized a lesson in epic history with modest success. He proved that he could adapt Homer with fidelity to the stage. His only serious mistake here was trying to stress love instead of valor. Love was one subject he never treated realistically in his longer plays, and the *Iliad* is hardly the place to look for it. Love in his longer plays is generally a weak, sentimental feeling treated very superficially, the love which is found in dreams but is of little use in daily life. Cruz did discover a way to make this kind of love moderately successful on the stage—in the form of the zarzuela. By setting his plot to music, he created an atmosphere in which this sentimental love and superficial idealism could be shown at their best. In *The Harvesting Girls* and in *The Gleaner*, Part One, he wrote plays which pleased the crowds and placed him at the head of the dramatists of his day. He even had a first in the zarzuela, as Cotarelo pointed out, that is, the first in giving native Spanish settings rather than Arcadian artificialities for his musical comedies. This is not to say that he made them realistic, but he at least took an important step in that direction.

The box office success was certainly a contributing factor to his persistence in writing these comedies and zarzuelas. The public, already predisposed in his favor as a result of the sainetes, was ready to attend and applaud these mediocre productions. Here we have another irony. Iriarte's fable proved to be true. The public accepted Don Ramón's plays because they were the best that were offered. Neither Iriarte nor any of his friends could offer them the dramatic food that they really wanted. If they accepted Don Ramón's straw, it was because his enemies were producing no succulent grain.

## V *Criticism and Influences*

Mr. Hamilton has an article, already cited, on Don Ramón's debt to Molière. The great French playwright was closer to the spirit of Ramón de la Cruz than were any of the other dramatists whose works he translated or adapted, and it is unfortunate that he had to reduce these adaptations to sainetes instead of giving them the full treatment that Molière gave them. For the others, Beaumarchais, Voltaire, Metastasio, Zeno, it would be too much to ask these dramatists to apologize for allowing their works to fall into Don Ramón's hands; he would have been better off if he had not wasted his time upon them. We should rather blame our playwright for not having given deeper thought to the nature of drama and that of his own talent, and add, as Galdós would have that the fault lay largely with the lack of genuine intellectual stimulation of the age in which he lived and wrote.

We have mentioned that the excesses of Napoleon's military policy gave the *petimetre* and *majo* society its coup de grâce. Ramón de la Cruz was not destined to have imitators. The sainete thus passed into history. Of course the one-act play, usually a farce, is still with us. Carlos Arniches has shown that Ramón de la Cruz is not the only Spanish dramatist who could build a lasting reputation upon the one-act play. The Quintero brothers brought sainete-like situations to plays of varying lengths. The spirit of the sainete recurs often in Spanish literature. For example, Camilo José Cela, in a story called *Timoteo el Incomprendido* (*Timothy the Misunderstood*), has quite suc-

cessfully embodied this spirit and technique, wisely using prose
for his vehicle. In this broader sense, the spirit of Don Ramón is
timeless. To paraphrase what Bécquer once said about poetry: As
long as man does not take himself too seriously to live, there will
always be farce, whether there is a comic writer to capture it or
not.

Those who tend to think that Don Ramón is overrated like to
call attention to the mediocrity of his verse. In this they are probably correct. Verse has certainly been important in Spanish
drama. Who can excel Lope de Vega in his command of such a
tremendous panorama of verse forms, all carefully applied to the
varieties of lyrical needs of his plays? José Zorrilla makes us
forget that he is a dramatist when we are absorbed with the
hypnotic effect of his lyrics. Yet I wonder how one would measure poetic beauty in a sainete. The language is so natural that
it sounds like prose. There are a few occasions in which a *cortejo*
has to make a pretty speech like that of the Golden Age *galán*,
and on these occasions, Don Ramón would have been more effective if he could have improved the lyric tone, although even here,
he would face a problem if he drew excessive attention to the
poetry when his main purpose is satire or burlesque. To put lyric
feeling into most of the speeches of the sainete seems out of
place, especially in a land that loves lyrics so well. It was a quality of the works of Gilbert and Sullivan in England to have
poetry that combined metric grace with loud laughter for the
ridiculous situation or thought that accompanied it. The same
technique might have been perilous in Spain, where lyricism can
combine the sacred and the profane, but probably not lyrical
splendor with banal lampooning thoughts. This indeed would
be sacrilegious.

Perhaps in a deeper sense which the critics never really describe, their accusations of Don Ramón's lack of lyricism are
correct. Except in a superficial way, he seems to lack any feeling
for the spiritual food of lyric poetry. The birds still sing in the
heart of Madrid in their daily salute to the dawn and their feeble
protest against the noise of gasoline-powered vehicles, but their
eighteenth-century ancestors did not inspire Don Ramón. He did
not really try to escape the bustle of Madrid life to seek the
plaintive note of the nightingale. He loved the big city noises.
He did not seek kinship with animals or other forms of nature

in a poetic pantheism. He was a quietly religious man, but no mystic fervor or anguish excited or tormented his soul. Marriage and a reasonable dowry were more significant for him than the despair of unrequited love. This lack of lyrical feeling helps explain the mediocrity of his pastoral plays; it is hard to see how it harms the sainetes.

The main differences of opinion noted in our previous chapter among the modern critics of Don Ramón have not really been due to fundamental differences in value judgments, but rather they represent varying weights to be placed upon the different literary qualities. All agree that Don Ramón wrote in a minor form. The best sainete cannot for its total impact be compared to the best tragedy or the best novel. Most of those who believe that Don Ramón is overrated stress his limitations. Those who believe that he is underrated emphasize how well he has performed in what he has striven to do.

## VI  *Conclusion*

To sum up briefly these thoughts on Ramón de la Cruz: The eighteenth century was the ebb tide of Spanish literature. The collapse of the old Spanish way of life, concomitant with the fall of the Austrian dynasty, and its replacement with the largely unassimilable French influence, casts a dark shadow between Spain's Golden Age and her nineteenth-century *risorgimento*. The light of Ramón de la Cruz burns brightly there, in part because there are few other lights to rival his. It is somewhat ironic that a writer of one-act plays could be considered one of the greatest literary figures of his age and perhaps the truest sustained expression of the national spirit. It is an injustice to Don Ramón and perhaps to his time as well, to think of him merely in this comparative light, for he has a skill that was unique, not only for his time, but for all Spanish literature. He had the talent for placing the life that he knew onto the stage, with complete honesty and with rare vividness. What he lacked in depth, he made up in spontaneity. What he lacked in sophistication and polish, he offered in comic genius and ingenuity. He takes his place in the parade of Spain's literary figures as proudly as the others, for those little sainetes, in their total impact, are almost a folk epic in the form of comic drama.

# Notes and References

## Preface

1. A typical theater program in eighteenth-century Spain consisted of a full-length play and several short skits, one before the play, one after, and one between each two acts. A sainete is a humorous short skit staged between the second and third acts of the feature play.

## Chapter One

1. As Agustín Durán put it in his edition of Don Ramón's sainetes: *Al consignar este hecho histórico tan triste y lamentable, no queremos ser ingratos a la Francia, que cuando el astro español quedó obscurecido, le prestó el reflejo de sus luces, e impidió que del todo se eclipsase del firmamento.* ("While we consider how sad and lamentable this historical event is, we must not be ungrateful to France, who, when the Spanish star was hidden by a cloud, lent her the reflection of its lights, thus preventing the total eclipse of the Spanish firmament.") (Ramón de la Cruz Cano y Olmedilla, *Colección de sainetes* (Madrid, 1843), p. 4.

2. Angel Valbuena Prat. *Historia de la literatura española* (Barcelona: Gustavo Gili, 1946), II, 492.

## Chapter Two

1. Emilio Cotarelo y Mori, *Don Ramón de la Cruz y sus obras* (Madrid, 1899), pp. 30, 32.

2. *Ibid.*, p. 228.

3. *Ibid.*, p. 231.

## Chapter Three

1. Cotarelo, *Don Ramón de la Cruz*, pp. 4–10.

2. We use the edition of Charles E. Kany, *Five Sainetes of Ramón de la Cruz* (Boston: Ginn and Company, 1926), pp. 3–39.

3. As mentioned above, the official name for the character is that of the actor—in this case—Ponce. Eusebio addresses Ponce as Don Alonso in the dialogue.

4. *Tertulia*, a party, usually one which convenes periodically with a relatively fixed guest list, if it is at a private home, or membership, if it meets at a cafe. For most of its history, conversation has been its focal point.

5. Olalla is the name that Joaquina calls Mariquita. See note 3.

6. Don Ramón puns on the two meanings of *duro*: "a coin" and "hard."

7. Teresa has been offered the cloth for four pesetas. She offers first two pesetas, then nine reales. Four reales equal one peseta. The duro is five pesetas.

8. *Hipocrás* is hippocras, a highly spiced wine.

9. Don Alonso is Ponce, as mentioned in note 3.

10. Antonio is Calderón; *Petimetra* is his wife.

11. At this point *Petimetra* dismisses Pegote. He does not leave the stage, but apparently withdraws enough for *Petimetre* to make his comment.

12. *Jácara*, a sprightly ballad featuring the *jácaro*, a merry braggart.

13. The Constable has previously used the handkerchief for storing gifts just as Ana has used her huge purses.

14. Occasionally it is difficult to follow Cruz's thought because of broken context. The best guess is that Ana is planning to ask Calderón for money when Campano interrupts. The Spanish text: "De hacer una diligencia que a vos solo la fiara, (*Llorosa*.) y eso con harta vergüenza. ¿Sabe usted quién será empeño . . .?"

15. Carretas Street: street of the public jail. It runs from the Puerta del Sol to the Plaza Benavente and so is just a few blocks away from the Plaza Mayor.

16. Chinica (sometimes Chinita) is Gabriel López, almost unquestionably the best of the comedians performing in the sainetes of Ramón de la Cruz. He was quite short and so his size frequently, though not here, is brought out in the dialogue.

17. In 1968 the Rastro remained as a market not very different from the one of the sainete. The Plaza Mayor had been torn up to make room for a huge parking area under the old Plaza. I understand that when the project is completed, the plaza will be restored. It is interesting to me that, while citizens of Madrid are comparable to others in their ignorance of their own history, they are unwilling to admit it. I asked a man who worked near the Plaza Mayor if he knew how many years it had been since the plaza ceased to be a marketplace. "It has never been," he replied. "But it was in the eighteenth century," I remonstrated. "No, Señor," he contradicted, "not then either."

18. Eusebio Rivera, producer and director of *The Results of the Fairs*, also acted in *The Main Square* and *The Rastro*.

## Chapter Four

1. *Nueva biblioteca de autores españoles* (Madrid, 1915), XXIII, 453.

2. This definition is introduced when one of the natives is puzzled by the word, *cortejo*, and asks, "What kind of fruit is that?" Don Ramón is probably punning on the word *corteza*, which means "peel." The fruit growing wild in the Prado, is a pun on the word, *prado*, which means "meadow," and also the name of the street where *cortejos* prowl. Ramón de la Cruz, *La civilización* in *Nueva biblioteca de autores españoles* (Madrid, 1915), XXIII, 98-99.

3. The Spanish word used here, *bata*, referred in Don Ramón's time to a formal dress.

4. The Spanish reads:

> *Don Fabricio ¡qué gracioso*
> *estaréis puesto de majo*
> *con su cofia, su chupita,*
> *chupetín y calzonazos,*
> *sus hebillas a la punta*
> *del pie, su capa arrastrando,*
> *su rejón en el bolsillo*
> *y en la boca su cigarro!*
> *Digo y para una pendencia*
> *¡qué mazo! con un gargajo*
> *fuerte que echara un chispero,*
> *se quedaría temblando.*

Ramón de la Cruz Cano, *El majo de repente* in *Colección de Sainetes*, Ed. Agustín Durán (Madrid, 1843), II, 209.

5. *Ibid.*, p. 215.

### Chapter Five

1. Translations of governmental titles can at best be approximations. The *corrgidor* as a direct representative of the king was likely to be a titled man and to have more power and social prestige than the leading local authority, the *alcalde*.

### Chapter Six

1. Don Ramón uses the spelling " 'Avapies," presumably to imitate the neighborhood's pronunciation. Barquillo Street was in the northeast sector of eighteenth-century Madrid; Lavapies Street and Square somewhat to the south. The rivalry between the two districts may have been only in Don Ramón's imagination. If they were comparable neighborhoods in his day, they are not today. As I saw them in 1968 Barquillo was a modern-looking street; Lavapies was still as poor as the name symbolizes: the annual Papal ceremony of washing the feet of the poor. Near Lavapies Square was a falling building, propped

uncertainly by huge stakes resembling a macabre parody of medieval flying buttresses and blocking the street to all motor traffic.

2. William A. Nitze and E. Preston Dargan, *History of French Literature* (New York, 1922), p. 315.

3. See Arthur Hamilton, "Ramón de la Cruz's Debt to Molière," *Hispania,* IV, 101-13.

4. *Puli(d)o* in Spanish means polished.

### Chapter Seven

1. With this manner of allowing the imagination free rein, I went (summer, 1968) to the corner of Belén and Barquillo Streets. Professor Kany reports this corner (*Five sainetes of Ramón de la Cruz* [Boston: Ginn and Co., 1926], p. xxviii) as the reputed site of the *casa de tócame Roque*. I found there a modern-looking store for fine cloth and tailoring. As I had learned to expect (see Chap. Three, note 17), when I asked a Spaniard within the store to confirm Mr. Kany's report, he replied that he had heard of the house; he did not know where it had been, but was sure that this was not the spot.

### Chapter Eight

1. Urbana: University of Illinois Press, 1926.

### Chapter Nine

1. According to Cotarelo, *Don Ramón de la Cruz,* pp. 266-67, the Eugénie of this play was Beaumarchais' sister and the Clarendon was the Spanish writer, José Clavijo y Fajardo.

2. *Ibid.,* p. 107. The printed version of the play (Barcelona: The Widow Piferer, n. d.) gives neither the author's nor the translator's name. Curiously enough, it states that the play is translated into Castilian from the English. The Spanish version provides phonetic equivalents for the English and Scottish names with the odd substitution of "t" for "f" as Freeport becomes Tripor. Faubrice and Falbrige (Montrose's friend, who does not appear) are both rendered by Fabricio in the Spanish. The Spanish version adds twenty percent to all financial transactions. While we can wish that we had definite proof that Don Ramón did indeed compose the translation, I can see no reason from the style to cast doubts upon Moratín's attribution of the translation to him.

3. *Ibid.,* p. 103.

4. Vallecas today is well inside Madrid. No place can be pointed to as the boundary connecting it to the rest of Madrid unless it is the Vallecas bridge which probably should be considered as outside the

section itself. New multistoried buildings are outside the tiny unit dwellings as if Madrid were symbolically squeezing the former suburb. Pinto is still several miles out, but along the road to Aranjuez, more large, moderately-priced apartments are being built to replace slums and perhaps within a few years Pinto, too, will be engulfed.

5. The tragedy of Inés de Castro has been written for the stage by many authors. According to Cotarelo, *Ramón de la Cruz,* p. 144, Don Ramón apparently had in mind *Agnes de Chaillot,* a parody that Legrand had made in 1723 on the *Inés de Castro* of M. de la Motte.

6. Cotarelo's attribution of this play to Racine is in two places: the bibliographic introduction of the *Nueva biblioteca de autores españoles,* Vol. 23, xxxiv, and the Appendix of Cotarelo's biography, *Don Ramón de la Cruz,* p. 256. In the biography, p. 105, he reported it was by Voltaire—almost certainly a slip. At that point (note 5) he says that he has not been able to examine Ramón de la Cruz's play. He adds that Cruz received fifteen hundred reales for it, the going price for original plays. Since Cruz busied himself during those years (performance 1769) in translating French and Italian plays, it is natural to assume that this play is a translation. Until it is proved to be a translation, we should leave open the possibility that Don Ramón is the original author. The play is not taken from Jean Magnon, *Le grand Tamerlan et Bajazet,* (Paris, 1648).

7. Cotarelo labels this play as Metastasio's. I have not been able to obtain the original or even a confirmation of Metastasio's authorship. From its structure, it is certainly plausible to attribute it to him.

8. Cotarelo, *Don Ramón de la Cruz,* p. 270. Chamfort's play takes place in Charleston, S.C., during the colonial period. The conflict matches love and gratitude against family, economic security, and tradition.

9. Cotarelo, *Don Ramón de la Cruz,* p. 118.

### Chapter Ten

1. Emilio Cotarelo y Mori, *Don Tomás de Iriarte y su tiempo* (Madrid, 1897), p. 255.

2. Cotarelo, *Don Ramón de la Cruz,* pp. 217-18.

3. *Ibid.,* p. 221.

4. Leandro Fernández de Moratín, *Obras,* in *Biblioteca de autores españoles* (Madrid, 1944), II, 317.

5. Ramón de la Cruz, *Colección* (Durán edition), p. 4.

6. Benito Pérez Galdós, "Ramón de la Cruz," *Memoranda* (Madrid, 1906), pp. 145-225.

7. Charles E. Kany, "Ramón de la Cruz," *Revue Hispanique,* LX, 40-185.

8. Arthur Hamilton, "Ramón de la Cruz's Debt to Molière," *Hispania*, IV, 101-13.

9. Arthur Hamilton, "Ramón de la Cruz, Social Reformer," *Romanic Review*, XII, 168-80. ,

10. *Historia del teatro español* (Barcelona: Montaner y Simón, editores, 1924), I, 320-24.

11. Valbuena, *Historia*, II, 499-502.

12. Richard E. Chandler and Kessel Schwartz, *A New History of Spanish Literature* (Baton Rouge: Louisiana State University Press, 1961), pp. 101-5.

# Selected Bibliography

## PRIMARY SOURCES

1. The one collection of his works made by Ramón de la Cruz is as follows: *Teatro o colección de los saynetes y demás obras dramáti- cas.* 10 vols., (Madrid: Imprenta Real, 1786–91). This collection contains forty-seven sainetes and nineteen of Don Ramón's other works. Relatively few copies of this edition are available. Their principal values to the researcher today are two: they are the only source of a number of the longer works, and they represent the author's judgment as to his most memorable productions. Almost all of the sainetes included are also available in more modern editions.

2. Collections of Cruz's works made by other persons are: *Colec- ción de los sainetes tanto impresos como inéditos de D. Ramón de la Cruz, con un discurso preliminar de D. Agustín Durán, y los juicios críticos de los Srs. Martínez de la Rosa, Signorelli, Moratín y Hartzen- busch* (Madrid: Yenes, 1843), dos volúmenes en 4° de XLVI-520 y 692 páginas. Called the Durán edition, it contains 120 sainetes.

*Nueva bilblioteca de autores españoles*, XXIII, XXVII (Madrid: Casa Editorial Bailly Baillière, 1915, 1928). The two volumes contain 163 sainetes and two other plays. Seventy-two of these are in the Durán edition. This edition, edited by Cotarelo y Mori, has a bibliography in the Introduction listing all known plays and per- formances, the edited plays including the editions, and the unedited, the location of the manuscripts.

KANY, C. E. (ed.). "Cinco sainetes inéditos de Ramón de la Cruz con otro a él atribuido," *Revue Hispanique*, LX (1924), 40-185.

———. "Ocho sainetes inéditos de Ramón de la Cruz (Berkeley: Univ. of California Publications in Philology, XIII [1925]), pp. 1-205.

———. *Five Sainetes of Ramón de la Cruz* (Boston: Ginn and Co., 1926). The five are *La plaza mayor, La pradera de San Isidro, Manolo, Las castañeras picadas, La Petra y la Juana.* This edi- tion has an Introduction, Notes, and Vocabulary, and offers a good beginning for studying Don Ramón.

SAINZ DE ROBLES, F., *Don Ramón de la Cruz, Sainetes* (Madrid: Aguilar, 1944). Fifteen sainetes in the Colección Crisol, a good edition for the general reader.

There are editions, too numerous to cite, of individual plays and sainetes, printed on cheap paper, usually with no cover at all, published in various cities of Spain, especially Barcelona and Valencia. Many of these appeared in the last decade of the eighteenth century and the first two decades of the nineteenth. Many do not carry the name of the author or the date of publication; some do not even name the publisher. Most of those that I have consulted have been examined in the library of the University of North Carolina or the Biblioteca Nacional of Madrid. In the case of several of those in Madrid, I had the honor of being the first reader; the pages had not been cut before my perusal of them.

## SECONDARY SOURCES

COTARELO Y MORI, EMILIO. *Don Tomás de Iriarte y su tiempo* (Madrid: Sucesores de Rivadeneyra, 1897). An important study of Don Ramón's time through the life and works of an adversary.

————. *Don Ramón de la Cruz y sus obras, ensayo biográfico y bibliográfico* (Madrid: Imprenta de José Perales y Martínez, 1899). The definitive biography. The appendices, longer than the text, give a wealth of documents, biographies of the actors and actresses who staged Don Ramón's plays, even sheet music from one of his zarzuelas.

PEREZ GALDOS, BENITO. "Ramón de la Cruz." *Memoranda* (Madrid: Perlado Páez y Compañía, 1906), pp. 145-225. An evaluation sympathetic to Don Ramón as a bulwark against the unsympathetic appraisal of eighteenth-century literature in Spain.

HAMILTON, ARTHUR. "Ramón de la Cruz's debt to Molière," *Hispania*, IV (1921), 101–13. The only article I have seen concerning Cruz's debt to anyone.

————. "Ramón de la Cruz, Social Reformer," *Romanic Review*, XII (1921), 168–80. Claim is made that Cruz consciously sought moral uplift through his plays.

————. *A Study of Spanish Manners from the Plays of Ramón de la Cruz* (Urbana: University of Illinois Press, 1926). Spanish manners, habits, and dress as the sainetes pictured them.

VEGA JOSE. *Ramón de la Cruz, poeta de Madrid* (Madrid: Sistemas de Control S. A., 1945). An almost novelized and poetized biography.

# Index